500 ROMANCE WRITING PROMPTS

-WORKBOOK-

Erica Blumenthal

500 Romance Writing Prompts: Workbook Edition/ Erica Blumenthal. -- 1st ed.
ISBN 978-0-6488502-4-3 (Print-Workbook)

To my readers - remember, it's never too late to start writing. Just start and don't look back.

CONTENTS

IINTRODUCTION...1

HOW TO USE THIS BOOK 3

    Romance Writing Tips 5

100 PARANORMAL ROMANCE PROMPTS 7

100 SCI-FI ROMANCE PROMPTS 67

100 ROMANTIC SUSPENSE PROMPTS 127

100 HISTORICAL ROMANCE PROMPTS 185

100 FANTASY ROMANCE PROMPTS 243

SUMMARY 301

CHAPTER ONE

IINTRODUCTION

I wrote this book for my readers who just love writing romance-writing prompts. I wanted to write a small book to supplement what's already available on Amazon and to help you focus in on romance writing specifically. This book is to help you if you're stuck, or to give you a prompt from which to start writing.

Writing prompts can be a great source of inspiration for when you're struggling for ideas. Even browsing the prompts can spark your own ideas for a story, or you can use the prompts exactly as they're presented.

Anything goes. And you get to decide!

You might be wondering about me; well, I've been writing since I was about eight years old. I love pretty much every genre including fantasy, sci-fi, adventure stories, and many of the sub-genres of romance, especially historical romance, and more recently contemporary romance.

I started my self-publishing career in the last 12 months, starting with *500 Fantasy Writing Prompts*, followed by launching my contemporary short romance pen name. I am also working on a YA Fantasy series (I'm still writing Book 1).

I love stories, especially creating new ideas. Ideas seem to come easily for me, I've realised. It's writing the full story that's hard. So here are some ideas for you, my reader, to help start, continue, or help finish your romance story.

Happy Writing!

CHAPTER TWO

HOW TO USE THIS BOOK

Here are some tips to help you use the prompts to your advantage. Remember - there are no rules when it comes to working with writing prompts.

1. Use the prompts to ignite an idea within you. You don't have to take them as is, just take what you like out of them, take the idea, character, anything that you can use as inspiration, to spark off your writing session.

2. Ask yourself questions if you're having trouble getting started... "Who is this character? What do they want? What do they need? What or who is standing in their way? What will happen if they don't get what they want/need?"

3. Aim to write 100 or 200 words or if you'd rather set a timer for 10 or 15 minutes or even 5 minutes and write to that, come what may.

4. Check out Holly Lisle's post on "writing to a writing prompt". Paraphrased, she says, you need to have a Character/Subject and a Conflict. From there, you can create any story you desire.

5. A way to use the prompts, if you are practicing regular writing, is to do one each day, for a set period, perhaps as a "writing exercise" to start of each writing session. Pick a section and start making your way down the list.

6. Try Freewriting. Flip through the book and choose a prompt at random and write it even you hate it. Your hesitation may prove to spark an excellent idea for a short story or something longer.

I have broken this book up into 5 sections including; Paranormal Romance, Sci-Fi Romance, Romantic Suspense, Historical Romance, and Fantasy Romance. I chose these sub-genres partly because they are easier for me to create prompts for, as I love speculative fiction and partly because of their popularity in the romance market right now.

Within each section there are two types of writing prompt:

1. The first set of prompts are titled "story starters" and indicate a style of prompt that typically contains a single line of text or dialogue, designed to spark a story in your mind or on the page within a timed writing exercise. These typically don't have a character or setting, but usually the conflict or situation. Again, it's then up to you to build out your story idea.

2.   The second set of prompts is your typical writing prompt, with typically a character, setting and a conflict. You might even get a villain for your protagonist. Sometimes one or more of these elements are missing. It's then up to you to create the missing pieces for your story idea.

Remember, for both style of prompt, take what you like, and disregard what you don't. You never have to use the prompts as is.

Romance Writing Tips

It was suggested that I provide a little more writing instruction for those of you just starting out. Now, I could provide a quick outline, however I really recommend following up with some key writing craft books, especially in the romance genre. At the end of this section, I provide a recommended reading list for story craft and romance writing.

There are many different ways to write, and there is no true one way. Every writer has to find their method (and annoyingly it can change between books and projects), which is tough, but there are many guides out there to help you through this process. Below I detail my favourite methods for starting and finishing a short story or novel, but remember, these are just the methods that work for me, and I'm just one person.

Following The Characters Method

I guess you could call this method pantsing. I find it's a great place to start, and it's super fun to do when you're writing from a prompt. But problems start (for me) if you don't quickly hone in on what your story is or wants to be after a few pages. The key here is to develop your main characters and find out what the conflict or situation is.

Once I have the main characters and their wants/ and needs and things getting in the way, the story can often write itself.

My Process:

1. I take a prompt I like, or hate, or a random one.
2. Set a timer – I like 8 or 10 minutes.
3. Start writing using the prompt as a starting point. I try to use all of the allotted time, and let anything come out – it doesn't have to be perfect.
4. After the writing session is finished, either right away or the next day, I'll review what I've written and think about what I've created. Then, I start asking myself questions. Do I have a character who I like? What is happening to them? Are they in a situation? What do they truly desire?
5. If I like the character, but not much is happening to them yet (i.e. conflict…i.e. story), then I take my character and just start brainstorming. I like lists, but any method of brainstorming is great, especially mind maps. Start with what your character really wants – then start brainstorming ideas of what could happen to stop her/him from achieving that goal. What's the worst possible thing that could happen to them Right Now? That there could be the major starting point of a short story or a novel. After the worst thing has happened, the rest of your story is how your character deals with it, still trying to reach his or her goal.
6. Simply put, my writing process goes:
   Character with a need/want->Disaster->Character responding to that Disaster.

Plotting Method

Using a little bit of forethought and plotting is great for romance stories because there are a few specific moments that typically need to happen in a romance story. These include the meet-cute, the moment when the two future lovers meet, and the happily ever after (or happily for now).

There is a most excellent guide for romance writers called *Romancing the Beat* by Gwen Hayes. A lot of romance writers I know swear by this book. But there is also another book, which I love, and is a bit simpler to get into: *Love Stories: Writing a Romance Novella in Thirty Days or Less* by Rachelle Ayala.

I highly recommend both of these books if you need a bit more structure to help guide your story while you write. Both books are available on Amazon on Kindle Unlimited.

You can write a great romance story without knowing the story structure information found in these books, but they do help you to create a story that readers will enjoy too.

Recommended Reading:

General Story/Outlining Books:
- *Save the Cat! Writes a Novel* by Jessica Brody
- *Story Engineering* by Larry Brooks
- *Structuring Your Novel* by K.M. Weiland

Romance Specific:
- *Romancing the Beat* by Gwen Hayes
- *Love Stories: Writing a Romance Novella in Thirty Days or Less* by Rachelle Ayala.

CHAPTER THREE

100 PARANORMAL ROMANCE PROMPTS

On the following pages are Romance Prompts falling under the general heading of Paranormal Romance. These are my favourite types of romance stories. In this section I've included prompts that involve Angels and Demons, and Vampires, Werewolves, and Shifters.

For each prompt, first think about:

Who is my character?
What is the setting?
What is the conflict?

50 Paranormal Romance Story Starters

1.   "It was Lana's first time on the other end of a werewolf claw, and surprisingly enough, fear was the furthest thing from her mind."

_____
_____
_____
_____
_____
_____
_____
_____
_____
_____
_____
_____
_____
_____
_____

2.   All of this fairy business was starting to get to him. It wasn't because he feared what the fairy Queen could do to him, he feared that he might like it.

_____

3.   Falling for the opposition's war chief was undoubtedly a mistake, but how could she resist those baby blue Elven eyes.

_____

4.   Right here in Limbo, she can finally feel the soft brush of his fingers on her cheek again. This isn't how she imagined their reunion, but she didn't regret it.

5.   Now, faced with the fear of losing the man who means everything to her, losing her newfound telekinetic abilities seemed like a walk in the park.

6.   They say love is a battlefield, but they never tell you about the war that wages when your wife is secretly a banshee.

_____

_____

_____

_____

_____

_____

_____

_____

_____

_____

_____

_____

_____

_____

_____

_____

_____

_____

_____

_____

_____

_____

_____

_____

_____

_____

_____

_____

_____

_____

_____

_____

_____

_____

_____

_____

7. Looking into his cat-like eyes now, she didn't see a monster. She saw the same kindness that brought this curse upon him in the first place.

8.   The vampire walked up to her with purpose in his stride. Through a haze, she reached out and softly brushed away the drop of blood from his lips.

_____
_____
_____
_____
_____
_____
_____
_____
_____
_____
_____
_____
_____
_____
_____
_____
_____
_____
_____

9.   Her mother had always raged about how their old house had been haunted, what she didn't expect was the ghost looking like an old-school Hollywood movie star.

_____
_____
_____
_____
_____
_____
_____
_____
_____
_____
_____
_____
_____
_____
_____

10. She could hear the trees whispering to turn back and run, but screw destiny. She knew of the man underneath the beastly exterior, and she loved him in spite of it.

11. She returned to her childhood home to find that everything was still the same. Well, everything except for the handsome man with the bright yellow eyes sitting on the sofa.

12. If some had told her a year ago that she'd be dating a vampire, she'd laugh in their faces. She bit back a smile. It's funny how life always takes an unexpected turn.

13. She dropped the ginger root in the cauldron and continued chanting the words from the silly book. The perfect boyfriend spell was supposed to be just a joke, so why was there a gorgeous naked man in her bed?

14. A strand of her hair caught on his wing as he wrapped his arms around her. So what if she was dating an angel, nowhere in the bible did it say that wasn't allowed!

15. Daniel tripped on a stray vine for the fifth time since he had entered the woods. Being with a nymph was proving to be much more trouble than he had initially thought.

16. She faced her attacker and was met with the wicked grin of a gorgeous bloodsucker. So help her god, she wasn't sure if she was supposed to kill him or kiss him.

_____
_____
_____
_____
_____
_____
_____
_____
_____
_____
_____
_____
_____
_____
_____
_____
_____
_____
_____
_____
_____
_____
_____
_____
_____
_____
_____
_____
_____
_____
_____
_____
_____
_____
_____
_____
_____

17. It seems the monster in the woods wasn't just a scary story her grandmother told her when she was young. In all of her retellings though, her grandmother missed the part about the wolfman having killer abs.

18. In the dead of night, all she could see was the red glow of dozens of eyes behind the trees. Then she spotted the one pair of dazzling emerald ones, and she knew they were the path to her salvation.

19. He stroked her sun-kissed hair as they lay in a heap near the pond. Of course, he'd fall for the only vampire that wasn't affected by the daylight, and he wouldn't have it any other way.

20. The reading on the EMF showed signs of a presence near the door. Was this the same spirit who's strong arms she could feel wrapped around her last night?

_____
_____
_____
_____
_____
_____
_____
_____
_____
_____
_____
_____
_____
_____
_____
_____
_____
_____

21. The flame on the candle died out, and they were left in complete darkness. In the deathly silence, she could hear him whisper to her. "You were always mine."

_____
_____
_____
_____
_____
_____
_____
_____
_____
_____
_____
_____
_____
_____
_____
_____
_____
_____

22. He wiped the smirk off his face with a well-executed high kick. He might be nature's most advanced predator, but she was always in control, at least when they weren't in bed together, anyway.

23. She barely made any traction as she forced herself to move through the swamp. Whatever that thing was, it wanted her, and at this point, she wasn't sure if that was a good or a bad thing.

24. Waking up with a sleeping elf in her bed wasn't on her agenda, but if her hunch was right, the man next to her was her best chance to make it into their world.

_____
_____
_____
_____
_____
_____
_____
_____
_____
_____
_____
_____
_____
_____
_____
_____
_____
_____

25. It was all on her now. She could use the silver dagger to pierce through the werewolf's heart and end it all, or she could take his hand and try her best not to break it again.

_____
_____
_____
_____
_____
_____
_____
_____
_____
_____
_____
_____
_____
_____
_____
_____
_____

26. He made a vow to avenge her death, but he didn't expect her to be with him for it every step of the way.

27. In all of the stories he'd heard, mermaids lured sailors to their death. At this moment, he thought death might be worth it just to feel her skin against his.

28. Her skin glistened in the moonlight as she took off her gown. This was the first time he'd seen her true form, and nothing could have prepared him for how beautiful she was.

---

29. It was an odd development. The little girl afraid of the monsters under her bed grew up to be a beautiful young woman who invites them into bed with her.

---

30. She could hear the screeching on the walls again as lay underneath her bedcovers. She wasn't afraid of him this time; in fact, she couldn't wait for the demon to jump into bed with her.

31. "I want you to stay" "If I stay they'll kill me. They don't take kindly to my kind around here." "Fine, then. I'm coming with you!"

32. Zeus, the almighty God of the skies, had asked her out. She wanted to say yes, but if all of those old myths about him were true, could she really trust such a player?

33. Her world was thrown in disarray. She and the new sexy vampire had been getting dangerously close, but on the other hand, her werewolf best friend had just confessed his feelings for her.

34. "You can come out now, she's gone." You whisper. The form slowly creeps out of the shadows, gently tips your chin up with its rough finger, and kisses you.

_____
_____
_____
_____
_____
_____
_____
_____
_____
_____
_____
_____
_____
_____
_____
_____
_____
_____
_____

35. "Just because I'm a sorceress doesn't mean you can use me to take care of your problems." She pouted angrily, but she knew that she'd do it again if it meant spending more time with him.

_____
_____
_____
_____
_____
_____
_____
_____
_____
_____
_____
_____
_____
_____
_____
_____

36. She hated him, he was a vampire, and she was a werewolf! They were natural-born enemies, so why did her heart skip a beat every time he smiled at her?

_____
_____
_____
_____
_____
_____
_____
_____
_____
_____
_____
_____
_____
_____
_____
_____
_____
_____

37. He breezed past her with superhuman speed, leaving her to pick up her jaw off of the floor. Great, on top of being in love with her best friend, she now had to deal with being in love with her genetically enhanced best friend.

_____
_____
_____
_____
_____
_____
_____
_____
_____
_____
_____
_____
_____
_____

38. She saw a flash of her future and was instantly paralyzed by fear. He wasn't in it, and she would challenge fate itself if she must in order to change that outcome.

_____
_____
_____
_____
_____
_____
_____
_____
_____
_____
_____
_____
_____
_____
_____
_____
_____
_____
_____

39. She took her best friend's hand and squeezed it to reassure him she wasn't going anywhere. It didn't matter that he was a vampire now; she could never stop loving him.

_____
_____
_____
_____
_____
_____
_____
_____
_____
_____
_____
_____
_____
_____
_____
_____
_____

40. Medusa took off her shades and approached the handsome man sitting on the park bench alone. Thank God for contact lenses, they truly made life a whole lot easier.

_____

_____

_____

_____

_____

_____

_____

_____

_____

_____

_____

_____

_____

_____

_____

_____

_____

_____

_____

_____

41. The troll that towered over her suddenly fell to the ground in a heap. As the monster crumbled, she caught a glimpse of him out of the corner of her eye. The demon she was hunting had saved her life, which certainly made things a lot more complicated.

_____

_____

_____

_____

_____

_____

_____

_____

_____

_____

_____

_____

_____

_____

_____

42. Now that she knew what she was capable of, Minerva laid out a plan to get the man of her dreams. All she needed now was a cauldron, some ginger root, and a drop of her future lover's blood.

43. She had been seeing him in her dreams for months now, and now he was really in front of her. Tongue-tied, she did what any respectable young witch would do; she cast a paralysis spell on the beautiful boy and ran in the opposite direction.

44. Agonizing over her now ex-boyfriend's affair, she decided she would start from scratch and make a new one, a better one.

45. As an Empath, she could always sense what others were feeling. With his hand on hers now, the only thing she could feel was the heat of a thousand suns burning her skin.

46. He reaches out to touch you, but you push him away. He's the future king of the underworld, and you... you're just a nobody from a small town in Minnesota.

47. Somewhere along the way in their little charade, she had truly started to fall for the angel that irritated her cold demon heart just a couple of weeks ago.

48. The sky turned black and ashes poured down from the endless abyss. Her husband was finally here, and she was more than ready to rain hellfire on this forsaken world right there by his side.

49. She never realized that witch blood was an aphrodisiac for vampires. If only she had known sooner, she and her best friend would have gotten together a long, long time ago.

50. She had never felt as alone as she did on the night she died. A lot has changed since then. Now she had two smoking hot necromancers fighting over who gets to be with her once they bring her back to life.

_____
_____
_____
_____
_____
_____
_____
_____
_____
_____
_____
_____
_____
_____
_____
_____
_____
_____
_____
_____
_____
_____
_____
_____
_____
_____
_____
_____
_____
_____
_____
_____
_____
_____
_____
_____

50 Paranormal Romance Prompts

1.   Write about a girl who performs a spell to bring her husband back to life after a car accident. The spell works, but the couple has to face the consequences of death wanting something in return.

_____

_____

_____

_____

_____

_____

_____

_____

_____

_____

_____

_____

_____

_____

_____

_____

_____

_____

_____

_____

2.   Write about a reporter who stumbles into a conspiracy about the government experimenting with creating lycanthropes for the military. During her investigation, she falls for one of the men being experimented on.

_____

_____

_____

_____

_____

_____

_____

_____

_____

_____

_____

_____

_____

_____

_____

_____

3. Write about a woman who falls in love with her cagy next-door neighbour in the span of a few months, only to discover he had been killed by the mob a few months ago and his spirit is tethered to his apartment.

4. Write about a girl who discovers her peaceful life on the secluded island she lives in is a front for government experimentation, and that she and her boyfriend have been groomed to be psychic field operatives with telepathic powers.

5.   Write about a lawyer who has to defend her handsome client in a murder trial. They fall in love during their time together and he reveals that he did in fact commit the murder, but the man he killed wasn't a man at all.

---

6.   Write about a con artist that falls for the man she's trying to swindle. She discovers he has a dark secret of his own, and ultimately has to make the choice of finishing her con or fighting to be with the vampire she's fallen for.

7. Write about an adrenaline junkie that stumbles into the kind of exciting adventure she's always dreamed of. The underground world of the supernatural syndicate is everything she could have asked for, but she questions if endangering her life is worth it when she meets a werewolf she can picture settling down with.

8.   Write about a necromancer whose lifespan is shortened every time she brings someone back from the dead. She reluctantly agrees to stop when she meets the love of her life, but it's not long before her true calling starts pulling her back into old and dangerous habits.

_____

_____

_____

_____

_____

_____

_____

_____

_____

_____

_____

_____

_____

_____

_____

_____

_____

_____

_____

_____

_____

_____

_____

_____

_____

_____

_____

_____

_____

_____

_____

_____

_____

_____

_____

_____

_____

_____

9. Write about a man who falls in love with a demon hunter after being attacked by a hellspawn. Their relationship is tested when he finds out he's half-demon himself, and his new girlfriend has to protect him from the bounty on his head.

_____

_____

_____

_____

_____

_____

_____

_____

_____

_____

_____

_____

_____

_____

_____

_____

_____

_____

10. Write about a conspiracy theorist that goes in search of a monster in the woods. He finds that the monster isn't at all what he expected, and chooses to stay with it instead of exposing it to the public.

_____

_____

_____

_____

_____

_____

_____

_____

_____

_____

_____

_____

_____

_____

_____

_____

_____

11. You just found out the one you love is an immortal being. Write about your search for immortality in mystical worlds in order to keep up with him.

_____
_____
_____
_____
_____
_____
_____
_____
_____
_____
_____
_____
_____
_____
_____
_____
_____
_____

12. Write about a witch that loses her powers when she's around the one she loves.

_____
_____
_____
_____
_____
_____
_____
_____
_____
_____
_____
_____
_____
_____
_____
_____
_____
_____

13. Write about a girl who goes to a university where the Greek houses are actually spearheaded by Greek gods as college students, and both Zeus and Hades are trying to win her heart.

14. Write about a girl who falls for the merman that saved her kid brother from drowning during a boating accident.

15. Write about a man torn between sticking to his family tradition of joining the police force or choosing a life of adventure when he meets an elf whose charms he can't resist.

16. Write about a girl who discovers her family is part of a coven of witches after gaining the ability to read minds. While running away from a group of witch hunters, she comes face to face with a young hunter that wants no part of his family's legacy.

17. Write about a girl who walks in on her boss while he's drinking the blood of a new intern. Instead of killing her, he introduces her to the hidden world of the vampire mafia.

_____
_____
_____
_____
_____
_____
_____
_____
_____
_____
_____
_____
_____
_____
_____
_____
_____
_____
_____
_____

18. Write about a group of friends who gain supernatural abilities after a surviving a car crash. They have to run from the military that wants to use them as guinea pigs, but along the way one of the girls falls in love with the agent after her.

_____
_____
_____
_____
_____
_____
_____
_____
_____
_____
_____
_____
_____
_____
_____
_____
_____

19. Write about a woman who has faked being a medium for monetary gain, up until one night she truly starts to see the dead and falls in love with the ghost of one of her widowed clients.

_____
_____
_____
_____
_____
_____
_____
_____
_____
_____
_____
_____
_____
_____
_____
_____
_____
_____

20. Write about a man who has to choose between indulging in his vampire girlfriend's murderous desires, or killing her and stopping her reign of terror.

_____
_____
_____
_____
_____
_____
_____
_____
_____
_____
_____
_____
_____
_____
_____
_____
_____

21. Write about a nanny who gets a job as a caretaker for the child of a hot single dad. She only sees her employer when she leaves at night, and one day when the baby bites her neck instead of its Binky, she realizes why.

_____
_____
_____
_____
_____
_____
_____
_____
_____
_____
_____
_____
_____
_____
_____
_____
_____
_____
_____
_____
_____
_____
_____
_____
_____
_____
_____
_____
_____
_____
_____
_____
_____
_____
_____
_____
_____
_____

22. Write about a girl who suspects her boyfriend is a murderer. One night she decided to follow him to prove her suspicions, only to find out that what he's killing isn't human at all.

23. Write about a troubled high school student that's infatuated with the school's resident bad boy. To her surprise, he asks her out, but she finds out he's involved with a satanic cult. What's more, he's the demon they've summoned.

_____

_____

_____

_____

_____

_____

_____

_____

_____

_____

_____

_____

_____

_____

_____

_____

_____

_____

24. Write about a girl who falls in love with her imaginary friend. Years later, when she returns to her childhood home, she realizes he isn't as imaginary as he seemed, and she still has feelings for him.

_____

_____

_____

_____

_____

_____

_____

_____

_____

_____

_____

_____

_____

_____

_____

_____

_____

_____

25. Write about a soldier who undergoes an experiment that turns him into a monstrous creature. With his appearance terrifying but his mind still intact, he tries to win back his wife and prove to her that he's the same person.

_____
_____
_____
_____
_____
_____
_____
_____
_____
_____
_____
_____
_____
_____
_____
_____
_____
_____
_____
_____

26. You wake up with majestic wings sprouting from your lower back. Write about your search for answers and the charming demon that helps you find them.

_____
_____
_____
_____
_____
_____
_____
_____
_____
_____
_____
_____
_____
_____
_____
_____
_____

27. The goth boy you like confesses to you that he's a vampire, but doesn't want to hurt anyone. Write about the way you help him secure donor blood and protect him from the werewolves that the vampires are at war with.

_____
_____
_____
_____
_____
_____
_____
_____
_____
_____
_____
_____
_____
_____
_____
_____
_____
_____
_____

28. Write about a psychic that mistakenly summons a demon prince instead of the spirit she's contacting. He makes it his goal to make her life difficult, but is secretly in love with her.

_____
_____
_____
_____
_____
_____
_____
_____
_____
_____
_____
_____
_____
_____
_____
_____
_____
_____

29. Write about a group of friends that go into the woods to see if the story about the wicked witch that lives there is real. The tables turn on them when one of the friends is revealed to be the witch's lover and is helping her pick them off one by one.

30. Write about a ghost that can pass through the veil between worlds and the girl that would do anything just to be with him.

31. Write about a single mom whose daughter is kidnapped by a pack of werewolves. She enlists the help of a paranormal investigator that helps her find her daughter and falls for him amidst all the action.

32. You've just been kidnapped by a vampire cabal for an unknown reason. Write about the devilishly handsome rogue member of the group that helps you escape their clutches.

33. Circe, the goddess of sorcery, had always toyed with humans, but this was the first time she had fallen for one. Write about her attempts to settle down and live with her human boyfriend in today's modern world.

34. The fates have quit their jobs and given you complete control over the wheel of fortune. Write about how you use the wheel to get everything you've always dreamed of, including the perfect partner, and the consequences of those actions.

35. Your tropical paradise vacation turns into a nightmare when a monstrous creature starts terrorizing the island. Write about your attempt to tame the beast and the deep connection you form when you're alone.

36. Write about a witch that's dating an ambitious warlock who shows her adventure and a down-to-earth werewolf who's ready to settle down at the same time.

37. Write about a girl whose best friends with an elf. She's been in love with him since she can remember, but he's set to marry another from a noble Elven family.

38. You wake up disoriented in a field of flames and brimstone. A handsome devil takes your hand and urges you to come with him if you want to make it out alive. Where does he take you?

39.   You're surrounded by heavy fog as you make your way to the secluded farm in the country. Suddenly, you hear a terrifying growl and a wounded werewolf jumps in front of you. Write about the relationship you develop as you nurse him back to health.

40.   Write about a sheriff who wakes up in a coffin and digs his way out of it. He goes back home to his wife but is soon killed again when he tries to protect her from a serial killer. He wakes up in a coffin again and has to dig his way out of it.

41. Write about a girl who gets her hands on a magic lamp so she can ask the genie for her three wishes. As soon as she lays eyes on him, she only has one wish on her mind.

42. You and your partner are wizards caught in an elven civil war. Write about your attempt to get the elves to reconcile and the Elven princess that's making you doubt your current relationship.

43. You and the leader of a rival vampire hang have been at each other's throats for as long as you can remember, but that all changes when instead of killing you in your moment of weakness he spares your life.

44. Write about a witch whose arch-nemesis is a vampire that goes to a rival school. They find they have a lot more in common than they thought when they're forced to work together to save both their schools from a demonic threat.

45. Write about a psychic with the ability to hear spirits. She falls in love with the voice of a man who has unfinished business on earth and starts researching the occult for ways to give him a material form.

_____

_____

_____

_____

_____

_____

_____

_____

_____

_____

_____

_____

_____

_____

_____

_____

_____

_____

46. She should have known that summoning an incubus to be her date for the wedding was a bad idea. The stupid demon couldn't take her eyes off of her the whole night, and if she gave in to temptation, she'd lose her powers forever.

_____

_____

_____

_____

_____

_____

_____

_____

_____

_____

_____

_____

_____

_____

_____

_____

47. "So it wasn't real? You just used me to get in my mother's good graces?" Her usually bright wings dimmed their glow. "It may have started that way, Princess, but we're way past that. You're the only thing on my mind now."

_____

_____

_____

_____

_____

_____

_____

_____

_____

_____

_____

_____

_____

_____

_____

_____

_____

_____

_____

_____

_____

_____

_____

_____

_____

_____

_____

_____

_____

_____

_____

_____

_____

_____

_____

_____

_____

_____

_____

_____

_____

48. "Wait, you're a demigod?" "I thought that was obvious." "Oh no no no, this is bad! I'm a demon, if I'm caught even talking to you I'll spend eternity in the seventh circle! I don't even want to know where they'll put me if they find out we've been sleeping together..."

_____
_____
_____
_____
_____
_____
_____
_____
_____
_____
_____
_____
_____
_____
_____
_____
_____
_____
_____
_____
_____
_____
_____
_____
_____
_____
_____
_____
_____
_____
_____
_____
_____
_____
_____
_____
_____
_____

49.   She cracked an eye open and watched the sunlight slip through the window and onto his curled wings. In theory, the love between an angel and a demon should be impossible, but somehow, they managed to make light and dark work in perfect harmony.

_____

_____

_____

_____

_____

_____

_____

_____

_____

_____

_____

_____

_____

_____

_____

_____

_____

_____

_____

_____

_____

_____

_____

_____

_____

_____

_____

_____

_____

_____

_____

_____

_____

_____

_____

_____

50. "You have to go through the window. If my dad sees you here, he'll kill you!" "Your dorm is on the fourth floor! I might be a demon but I can't just magically sprout wings." "Well, you're going to have to. He just texted he's on our floor."

Notes

_____
_____
_____
_____
_____
_____
_____
_____
_____
_____
_____
_____
_____
_____
_____
_____
_____
_____
_____
_____
_____
_____
_____
_____
_____
_____
_____
_____
_____
_____
_____
_____
_____
_____
_____
_____
_____
_____
_____

CHAPTER FOUR

100 SCI-FI ROMANCE PROMPTS

On the following pages are all sorts of Sci-Fi Romance story ideas and prompts. Here you'll find story ideas of Time-Travel, Space Opera, Space Pirates, and Alien and Human love matches.

For each prompt, first think about:

Who is my character?
What is the setting?
What is the conflict?

50 Sci-Fi Romance Story Starters

1.   You're mesmerized by the alien's shimmering body and step closer to him. He's caught off guard at first but with a dazzling smile as bright as his skin he steps closer as well.

_____
_____
_____
_____
_____
_____
_____
_____
_____
_____
_____
_____
_____
_____
_____
_____
_____

2.   Your ship's thrusters are blown to smithereens and your weapons system has gone haywire. Still, looking back to your gorgeous co-captain, you regret nothing.

_____
_____
_____
_____
_____
_____
_____
_____
_____
_____
_____
_____
_____
_____
_____
_____
_____
_____
_____
_____

3.   She expected to find signs of extraterrestrial life in the new colony, but she didn't expect them to swoop in and leave her breathless.

_____
_____
_____
_____
_____
_____
_____
_____
_____
_____
_____
_____
_____
_____
_____
_____
_____

4.   It suddenly hits you. You're smiling like a lunatic in your bed while texting your alien crush. Your senior year of high school has really taken a turn for the unexpected.

_____
_____
_____
_____
_____
_____
_____
_____
_____
_____
_____
_____
_____
_____
_____
_____
_____
_____
_____

5.   The fierce warrior from the new world you just crash-landed in gives you a menacing glare. You can't help but blush, she's cute when she's angry.

_____
_____
_____
_____
_____
_____
_____
_____
_____
_____
_____
_____
_____
_____
_____
_____
_____

6.   You've followed the instructions to a T but there's still nothing in the pod. You bow your head in disappointment when suddenly you hear a click and turn around to a very naked alien smiling from beneath the glass.

_____
_____
_____
_____
_____
_____
_____
_____
_____
_____
_____
_____
_____
_____
_____
_____
_____
_____

7.   You can't help but smirk at the striking resemblance between them. You definitely have a type, but should you tell your boyfriend you unknowingly hooked up with his brother on your last space mission?

_____
_____
_____
_____
_____
_____
_____
_____
_____
_____
_____
_____
_____
_____
_____
_____

8.   She flung herself over the railing and took out the guard with a well-executed chokehold. Her boyfriend winked at her from the other side of the spaceship, proud of her for picking up the moves he taught her so quickly.

---

9.   For a minute you wonder if the teleportation chamber is just taking too long, but then you realize it's done for. That was your last means of escaping the strange planet where you're set to marry the ascending king.

10. You're stuck in an escape pod in the middle of nowhere, with just your phone, and single contact on it... Your ex.

11. She stands up abruptly and storms out of the room. If only they looked past her boyfriend's four arms, they'd see that he also has two hearts.

_____
_____
_____
_____
_____
_____
_____
_____
_____
_____
_____
_____
_____
_____
_____
_____
_____
_____
_____
_____
_____
_____
_____
_____
_____
_____
_____
_____
_____
_____
_____
_____
_____
_____
_____
_____
_____

12. When her cellmate told her they'd been abducted by aliens she imagined little green men and weird crop circles, not the gorgeous guard that stood in front of their cage.

13. As a covert operative for the Raptor 1, flirting was one of her most effective weapons. This was the first time someone had resisted her charms, and now she made it her mission to get the elusive smuggler to fall for her.

14. The plants on earth 57 weren't like anything she had ever seen before, and soon, she would find out that neither were the world's smoking hot residents.

_____
_____
_____
_____
_____
_____
_____
_____
_____
_____
_____
_____
_____
_____
_____
_____
_____
_____
_____

15. You're distracted from trying to break into the enemy ship's mainframe by a holographic message from your wrist communication device. It's the evil, yet very handsome captain of their fleet, and wait, is he winking at you?

_____
_____
_____
_____
_____
_____
_____
_____
_____
_____
_____
_____
_____
_____
_____
_____

16. It was hard for her to believe that her gangly and awkward best friend had grown into one of the finest pilots in the galaxy. It was even harder for her to believe that she might be falling hopelessly in love with him.

_____
_____
_____
_____
_____
_____
_____
_____
_____
_____
_____
_____
_____
_____
_____
_____
_____
_____
_____

17. She pulled out her gun, took aim, and shot her husband right in the face. The man crumpled to the ground, his form shifting into a green blob spread out on the floor. She'd recognize her husband anywhere; these shape-shifting alien freaks weren't fooling her.

_____
_____
_____
_____
_____
_____
_____
_____
_____
_____
_____
_____
_____
_____
_____
_____
_____
_____

18. A knock on her door alarmed her. The only people up at the garrison at these hours were the supervisors and their extraterrestrial guests, and she'd been having a fling with one of each!

19. If love between humans and aliens was supposed to be unimaginable, why did their bodies fit together like perfect puzzle pieces?

20. She knew that time travel would be a tricky thing to navigate, but her boyfriend's dad and his brother competing for her love were at the bottom of her list of potential scenarios.

21. On top of her supervisor treating her like a child, Nina's new mission in the Andromeda galaxy is going to be led by none other than her ex. That's three weeks alone with two men she has a love/hate relationship with. What could go wrong?

_____
_____
_____
_____
_____
_____
_____
_____
_____
_____
_____
_____
_____
_____
_____
_____
_____
_____
_____
_____
_____
_____
_____
_____
_____
_____
_____
_____
_____
_____
_____
_____
_____
_____
_____
_____
_____
_____
_____
_____

22. As the crowds gather to gaze upon the first star-filled sky in over a century, the only thing he has eyes for is the woman standing next to him.

_____
_____
_____
_____
_____
_____
_____
_____
_____
_____
_____
_____
_____
_____
_____
_____
_____
_____

23. The alien invaders might have advanced tech and fancy weapons, but she has her trusty knife and the love of her life by her side. That's more than she needs to take them down.

_____
_____
_____
_____
_____
_____
_____
_____
_____
_____
_____
_____
_____
_____
_____
_____
_____
_____

24. The predatory race of aliens they've run into is like nothing they've ever seen before. Luckily, her team consists of the best fighters in the galaxy, including the new recruit who clearly knows how to handle himself both in and out of the bedroom.

_____
_____
_____
_____
_____
_____
_____
_____
_____
_____
_____
_____
_____
_____
_____
_____
_____
_____
_____

25. The long-term effects of travelling between dimensions were starting to weigh on her. If she kept going at this rate, even her husband wouldn't be able to recognize what she's become.

_____
_____
_____
_____
_____
_____
_____
_____
_____
_____
_____
_____
_____
_____
_____
_____

26. "I don't think she saw us." "She just made a snarky comment about interspecies relations while looking me dead in the eye. I'm pretty sure she saw us."

_____

_____

_____

_____

_____

_____

_____

_____

_____

_____

_____

_____

_____

_____

_____

_____

_____

_____

27. She realizes the spaceship is out of fuel and slams her fists on the controls in frustration. If she doesn't find a station nearby she'll never make it in time to stop the man she loves from making a huge mistake - marrying a woman he doesn't love.

_____

_____

_____

_____

_____

_____

_____

_____

_____

_____

_____

_____

_____

_____

_____

_____

_____

28. She was created in a lab to wipe out the last of the Martians hiding out in earth, but the gentle being in front of her is nothing like what the scientist had described.

_____
_____
_____
_____
_____
_____
_____
_____
_____
_____
_____
_____
_____
_____
_____
_____
_____
_____
_____

29. The chaos of explosions and laser beams surrounded her but she couldn't seem to give a damn. She had been waiting for an adventure like this her whole life, and to her surprise, her boyfriend had kept his promise and provided it to her.

_____
_____
_____
_____
_____
_____
_____
_____
_____
_____
_____
_____
_____
_____
_____
_____
_____

30. "Are you sure about this?" She asked the handsome Martian. They'd just met an hour ago, but she felt like she could trust him with her life. "I'm not, but it's the only thing I can think of that might get us out of this frozen hell hole alive."

_____

_____

_____

_____

_____

_____

_____

_____

_____

_____

_____

_____

_____

_____

_____

_____

_____

_____

31. He can see the intergalactic city of Lumis shining bright in the distance, and that palace right in the middle of it, that's where he needs to go if he wants to get the girl of his dreams back.

_____

_____

_____

_____

_____

_____

_____

_____

_____

_____

_____

_____

_____

_____

_____

_____

32. The machine purrs to life and suddenly he finds himself in a house he can barely recognize. He did it, he time traveled! All he needed to do now was to find the past version of his wife and tell her to stay as far away from him as possible.

_____

_____

_____

_____

_____

_____

_____

_____

_____

_____

_____

_____

_____

_____

_____

_____

_____

_____

33. She grabs her gun and points it at the alien's head. It watches it with curiosity, smiling brightly at her and reaching out to give her a hug.

_____

_____

_____

_____

_____

_____

_____

_____

_____

_____

_____

_____

_____

_____

_____

_____

_____

34. If she was going to be stuck in the 50s until her time travel device recharged, she'd at least have some fun with the dapper gentleman offering to buy her a drink.

35. Every time she looked out the balcony to her beautiful kingdom she felt the loneliness creeping in. What good was being this galaxy's queen if she had no one to share it with?

36. Now that space travel's opened up the possibility of travel to new worlds, you're about to embark on a journey to find the one thing you could never seem to find on earth - true love.

_____
_____
_____
_____
_____
_____
_____
_____
_____
_____
_____
_____
_____
_____
_____
_____
_____
_____

37. It's Elle's 21st birthday tomorrow, which means she finally gets her first spacecraft. With her secret crush and dorky best friend in tow, she's decided to journey to the Frozen Planet of Glacious, the last place her mother had been seen before she went missing.

_____
_____
_____
_____
_____
_____
_____
_____
_____
_____
_____
_____
_____
_____
_____
_____
_____

38. "Are you going to finish that?" The cute alien asked her with a dopey grin. "Humans can't eat Finnean food, help yourself!" She couldn't help but return a smile. She was falling for her new crewmate hard and fast, she only hoped it wouldn't compromise their recovery mission.

_____
_____
_____
_____
_____
_____
_____
_____
_____
_____
_____
_____
_____
_____
_____
_____
_____
_____

39. He carefully put the last piece of the crystal in its place, completing the artifact that was supposed to grant him everything he'd ever dreamed of. A blinding light surrounded the crystal, and a gorgeous blue woman emerged from the light, resting a hand on his shoulder.

_____
_____
_____
_____
_____
_____
_____
_____
_____
_____
_____
_____
_____
_____
_____

40. Working as a bartender on a galaxy explorer was exciting enough as it is, but when their ship was attacked and the irresistible space pirates asked her to join his crew in their adventures, life got a hell of a lot more interesting.

41. The predictive algorithm she developed with the help of her Android partner was working incredibly well. At this rate, she'd have her crush head over heels for her within the next week.

42. "Why didn't you run away like everyone else?" The alien asked with hope in his eyes. "It's just a few extra limbs and a different skin tone, Leon. If anything, I love you even more now that you've shown me your true self."

_____

_____

_____

_____

_____

_____

_____

_____

_____

_____

_____

_____

_____

_____

_____

_____

_____

_____

43. The dangers of space travel, aliens, and advanced weaponry never scared her, but the thing she felt when she thought she was going to lose him, that scared the daylights out of her.

_____

_____

_____

_____

_____

_____

_____

_____

_____

_____

_____

_____

_____

_____

_____

_____

_____

44. Meeting with alien ambassadors from different species was nothing out of the ordinary for her. What did strike her as odd was the way this Lorthrax peacekeeper was looking at her like she was his next meal, and she had to admit, she kind of liked it.

45. Living with a shape-shifting alien roommate was hard enough already, but now that he had changed his hair colour, eye colour, and body type; Inna couldn't help her thoughts from straying into dangerously sexy territory.

46. She wasn't sure if the energy prison she was being kept in was for her protection or theirs, but if she didn't get out soon she'd definitely be late for her date with her new commanding officer.

47. Her new genetic modifications made it harder for her to see until she got better adjusted to them, but even with her impaired vision it was clear that the new doctor working on making her the perfect weapon was very easy on the eyes.

48. "You've never been opposed to dating an alien before..." "Well, he's the exception!" "Is this really about him being an alien, or are you just scared of letting someone back in after what happened with Josh?"

49. His piercing red eyes made her stomach do a back flip. Falling for the alien bad boy was sure to be nothing but trouble, but she just couldn't resist a leather jacket and a bad attitude.

50. The enemy fleet was getting too close for comfort. She ordered her boyfriend to engage the weapons system and try to take out at least a dozen of them so they could engage warp speed. She trusted his skill, but if he managed to pull off this miracle, he'd definitely be in for a big treat the minute they get to safety.

50 Sci-Fi Romance Prompts

1. Write about a girl who finds a doorway to an alternate reality in her basement. Seemingly everything is different there, except the mysterious new boy who transferred to her school last month.

_____

_____

_____

_____

_____

_____

_____

_____

_____

_____

_____

_____

_____

_____

_____

_____

_____

2. Write about a girl who discovers the key to cloning. Her clones seem to have minds of their own, until they unexpectedly merge with her and she's left with foreign memories and three boys vying for her attention.

_____

_____

_____

_____

_____

_____

_____

_____

_____

_____

_____

_____

_____

_____

_____

_____

3. Write about the rise of two warring space empires and the two royals that brokered peace between worlds thanks to their love for each other.

---

4. Your boyfriend goes missing along with a few other people from your small town. Write about how you single-handed took down the aliens that abducted them and saved your boyfriend before they used him for their experiments.

---

5.   You're hunted by an unknown assailant but a mysterious man saves your life. Write about the secret organization he works for, the developing feelings between the two of you, and the mysterious alien relic that your mother left you before she died.

6.   Write about a girl who tries to broker peace with the aliens invading the earth. She falls for the alien representative they send but they have to keep it a secret if they want to bring their people together.

7.   Write about two opposing teams of space pirates who have to work together to save their home planet. Along the way, the two captains fall for each other.

———————————————————
———————————————————
———————————————————
———————————————————
———————————————————
———————————————————
———————————————————
———————————————————
———————————————————
———————————————————
———————————————————
———————————————————
———————————————————
———————————————————
———————————————————
———————————————————
———————————————————

8.   Write about a lonely old woman who travels back in time to her early twenties. Now knowing the mistakes she made back then, she focuses on pursuing the charming young man she fell for instead of her career as a lawyer that brought her nothing but pain.

———————————————————
———————————————————
———————————————————
———————————————————
———————————————————
———————————————————
———————————————————
———————————————————
———————————————————
———————————————————
———————————————————
———————————————————
———————————————————
———————————————————
———————————————————
———————————————————
———————————————————
———————————————————

9. Write about a man from the first alien colony that seeks refuge on earth. He grows to hate humans as they treat the aliens like dirt, up until a striking young human woman changes his mind that is.

10. Write about an astronaut on an exploratory mission to Mars. He finds exactly what he's looking and more when he stumbles upon an alien civilization lead by a Martian queen that he can't look away from.

11. Write about the warring worlds of Lyenn, led by Alana, and Ryalis led by Loki. In the heat of battle, the two leaders end up trapped below the surface of a dead planet, discovering hidden depths about each other, and the unexpected truth about the origins of their people.

12. Write about a singer on a luxury cruise spaceship. She starts hitting it off with a handsome traveler after one of her performances, but their flirting is cut short when mercenaries board the ship looking for her incredibly wealthy date.

13. You wake up in a parallel universe where everyone's gender is reversed except yours. Write about how you develop feelings towards your newly male best friend, and the conflicting emotions that come with the whole crazy shebang.

14. Write about a single mother who's abducted by aliens. She pleads with one of the handsome, but troubled, guards that has a soft spot for her, convincing him to let her go and join her on earth.

15. Write about an alien that can distort reality. He's been living his whole life in his own little world, up until the moment, he meets a girl who makes him see that even reality has its perks.

_____

_____

_____

_____

_____

_____

_____

_____

_____

_____

_____

_____

_____

_____

_____

_____

_____

_____

_____

16. Write about a training facility for young spaceship captains. The third-year Luna has kept the highest score on the simulator since her start there, but the cocky new first-year student she's been flirting with is getting dangerously close to beating it.

_____

_____

_____

_____

_____

_____

_____

_____

_____

_____

_____

_____

_____

17. Write about a time machine that can only be powered by the strongest of emotions. Emma recently lost her brother, and the love between her and her boyfriend is the last hope she has of getting him back.

18. Write about a parallel universe where people's wildest dreams run free. In a bar where two aliens spill about their dating troubles to a bartender, something no could have expected suddenly walks in - a beautiful human woman.

19. Write about an alien overlord that falls in love with one of the human subjects he's enslaved. His plans were to wipe the earth out of existence altogether, but will she be able to convince him that humanity's worth saving?

20. Write about a scientist who creates a drug that can bring people back from the dead. She tests it on herself, but when it seemingly stops working after the third time, can her hopelessly in love assistant come up with a way to bring her back in time.

21. The army's new motto is "the only good alien is a dead alien". Write about a human soldier that starts to question his orders after falling for one of the timid aliens he had once hunted.

22. After something goes wrong with your time machine, you end up with three different versions of yourself - the good, the bad, and the ugly. Write about your crazy attempt to piece yourself back together with the help of the machine's original inventor - your spouse.

23. Write about a girl who's very vocal about her hatred of aliens because of their special abilities, but is secretly in love with her telepathic alien neighbour who knows exactly what she thinks about him.

24. Write about a girl whose obsession with aliens leads her to Area 51. She releases the different alien species imprisoned by the government, but while she can imagine spending her life with one of them in particular, she's not sure the rest have the best intentions.

25. Write about Andoria, the biggest melting pot in the galaxy. There, a thief from the slums tries to steal from the royals and give back to the community. She finds an unlikely ally in a handsome prince who's sick of the monarchy.

26. She watches in horror as the ship carrying the man she loves spins out of control and straight into a black hole. Write about her crazy plan to get him back with the help of her estranged sister.

27. The ball drops and as the humans below celebrate the New Year, an alien fleet above prepares their forces for an invasion. Write about a girl who fights for survival, finds love, and discovers her inner warrior during New York's wildest New Year's celebration yet.

28. In the year 2084 where technology has advanced beyond our wildest imagination, write about a girl who refuses for an algorithm to choose who she spends the rest of her life with, and goes on a trip around the globe to find the love of her life the old-fashioned way.

29. Write about two clones that fall in love with the same man. Will he choose one of them, or run in the opposite direction when he finds out he's been dating two separate women?

30. Write about a device that allows people to peek into their future. A lonely man uses it to give himself hope, and he finds it in a woman he's now desperate to track down.

31. Write about a meteor that lands near an old loner's house. He regains his youth for short periods when he touches it, but what happens when he falls for a young woman that doesn't know his secret?

_____
_____
_____
_____
_____
_____
_____
_____
_____
_____
_____
_____
_____
_____
_____
_____
_____
_____

32. Write about an alien who can't feel emotions. He's moved through a world of gray his whole life, but when he meets a human for the first time his bleak world starts to fill with colour.

_____
_____
_____
_____
_____
_____
_____
_____
_____
_____
_____
_____
_____
_____
_____
_____
_____
_____

33. Write about a woman who doesn't believe in true love, up until the moment she finds herself on the intergalactic version of The Bachelorette.

34. Write about a girl who finds out her boyfriend is a Martian spy sent on earth to gather intelligence for their next invasion.

35. Write about a girl who steals an alien ship and pilots it to a new world. She realizes she's not alone on the vessel but is the handsome alien abroad a friend or a foe?

36. Write about an alien emperor who wages war against everyone who refuses to serve under his kingdom. He's cold and ruthless, but can the new human prisoner he's attracted to tap into a different side of him.

37. Write about a girl who can travel back in time but she can only visit the most disastrous moments in history. One day she finds herself in the Chernobyl disaster zone and falls for one of the scientists responsible, but is it really her place to change the course of history because of a crush?

38. Write about a girl who joins the intergalactic police force after her parents are killed in a robbery. She and her seasoned partner get into a few tussles during her first year on the job, but the real trouble she's facing is her developing feelings towards him.

39. Write about the first joint school for humans and aliens. Tensions between the two races are high, but can the budding love between two second-year students make them see that they aren't so different after all?

40. After our planet becomes uninhabitable, the remaining humans move to a massive space station. Write about a girl from the poorer sections that falls for the son of the station's leader.

41. Write about a group of people who come back to earth centuries after it was devastated by nuclear warfare. They find that by some miracle it's still inhabited, and a girl from the group can't help but follow one of the earth's beautiful survivors.

42. Write about a girl that hijacks a spacecraft so she can save her boyfriend who's been taken by an aggressive race or shape-shifting aliens.

43. Write about a shape-shifting alien who falls in love with her human best friend. She tries to change her looks so she can get him to like her, but along the way finds out that it's more important to stay true to herself than change for someone else.

_____
_____
_____
_____
_____
_____
_____
_____
_____
_____
_____
_____
_____
_____
_____
_____
_____
_____
_____
_____

44. Write about the leader of the resistance who along with her scrappy team of survivors tries to get rid of the alien invaders. She tries not to get too attached to anyone but realizes that love and hope are inseparable when she starts developing feelings for one of the other survivors.

_____
_____
_____
_____
_____
_____
_____
_____
_____
_____
_____
_____
_____
_____
_____
_____
_____
_____

45. Write about a girl whose strict parents don't let her date. What happens when they find out that not does she only have a boyfriend but her boyfriend's an alien?

46. Your pleasant coffee date with a cute actor is interrupted when the sky turns dark and fills with thousands of alien spaceships. Write about you and your date's attempt to survive the invasion in the crowded streets of LA.

47. Your dating app sets you up with a cute android that lives nearby. Write about your date taking a turn for the worst when the android's system is corrupted by a virus and he tries to take over the world.

48. Write about a genius girl who has trouble finding love, so instead of going on random dates that could go bust she creates the perfect AI robot boyfriend.

49. Write about a team of thieves that explore the galaxy, looking for new worlds full of riches. They hit the jackpot when they land on the crystal planet Lumen, but when their leader falls for a beautiful local he has to either confess he's a thief and potentially lose her or leave without saying anything and forever live with regret.

50. You and your best friend are about to go all the way to the floating City on Mars because of a girl you matched with on a dating app. Write about the hilarity that ensues.

_____
_____
_____
_____
_____
_____
_____
_____
_____
_____
_____
_____
_____
_____
_____
_____
_____
_____
_____
_____
_____
_____
_____
_____
_____
_____
_____
_____
_____
_____
_____
_____
_____
_____
_____
_____
_____
_____
_____

CHAPTER FIVE

100 ROMANTIC SUSPENSE PROMPTS

This section includes Romantic Suspense prompts. Here, I included prompts that involve more modern and suspenseful ideas and themes, such as mysteries, serial killers, and a lot of dead bodies.

For each prompt, first think about:

Who is my character?
What is the setting?
What is the conflict?

50 Romantic Suspense Story Starters

1. Anna walks back into her suite to find a dead body on the floor. With her exotic island vacation ruined and the police stumped on what to do next, she decides to take matters into her own hands. Unfortunately for her, all signs point to the handsome native she's been talking to since she arrived, but is he really capable of murder?

_____
_____
_____
_____
_____
_____
_____
_____
_____
_____
_____
_____
_____
_____

2.   When mild-mannered Mona wakes up in a strange apartment feeling hazy she immediately springs into action and rushes out of there. A confused coffee shop owner sees her distraught state and helps her out, but can the two of them find out what happened to Mona when one is clearly hiding ulterior motives?

3.   Her boyfriend's been knocked out cold and there's a killer donning a clown mask on her tail. The situation they've gotten themselves in might have started out as a silly mystery game but now she wondered if some things are better left buried.

4.   Six dead bodies washed ashore in less than a month and still no evidence pointing to who might have done it. When the department gets desperate and pairs detective Steele with a psychic who claims he can talk to one of the victims, she's not sure whether to punch the guy that's clearly running a scam or run her hands through his ridiculously perfect hair.

---

5.   On the run from the police, Hanna turns to the one person she never thought she'd see again for help - her bad boy ex-boyfriend. Someone's trying to set her up for murder, and between their steamy flirting and tumultuous past, maybe going to her ex wasn't the best idea.

---

6. With her abusive ex on the loose, Erica decides the best way to keep herself safe is by hiring some personal security. The problem is, the only guy she could afford to hire is as sketchy as he's good looking, and god knows what kind of problems that'll bring.

_____

_____

_____

_____

_____

_____

_____

_____

_____

_____

_____

_____

_____

_____

_____

_____

_____

_____

7. Allan knew Leah had baggage when they started dating, but the brutal scene he had just witnessed wasn't even close to what he was expecting.

_____

_____

_____

_____

_____

_____

_____

_____

_____

_____

_____

_____

_____

_____

_____

_____

_____

_____

8. In a twisted way, it was funny how a serial slasher had gotten loose on Halloween. What he didn't find funny though was the fact that he was after the girl he loved.

---

9. Sure, the circumstances weren't great, but what better time to tell your hot neighbour that like her than when you're both hiding behind a washing machine because your building is now the battlefield for a gang war?

---

10. If she tried to jump over to the next building, she'd probably fall and die. If she didn't, both she and her boyfriend would probably get kidnapped and killed. At least this way if she survives, she can come back with a loaded arsenal, take down these assholes, and hopefully get her boyfriend back alive.

11. She knew that she'd end up on the news someday one way or another, but she never thought it'd be as a prime murder suspect. To make matters worse, the only guy she ever loved was assigned to her case - her detective ex-boyfriend.

12. The water was deep enough so she could dive under it to hide. When she finally gave up and went up gasping for air, she ended up face to face with him. "Jesus Christ I thought you were the killer!" She hugged her boyfriend in relief. "I just ditched him, but I don't think he'll stay away for long."

13. Finding a dead body in a water tank was kind of a cliche, but that's how Reagan ended up being a suspect in a vicious murder. Through it all, her boyfriend had been her biggest support, but when she finds the victim's jacket in his drawer, she starts questioning everything.

14. The days when things were easy were long gone now. She chose him knowing the kind of things he did, and now every day she was a police chase away from spending the rest of her life rotting in a jail cell.

_____
_____
_____
_____
_____
_____
_____
_____
_____
_____
_____
_____
_____
_____
_____
_____
_____
_____

15. The ghost stories everyone shared at the campfire had truly spooked her, but there was no way she imagined the creepy figure in a bunny mask sneaking behind the trees. Her friends had laughed and called her crazy, but luckily her boyfriend was by her side to keep her safe.

_____
_____
_____
_____
_____
_____
_____
_____
_____
_____
_____
_____
_____
_____
_____
_____
_____
_____

16. She's drowning, and then suddenly, someone pulls her out of the water and rushes her to the beach. Her beautiful lifeguard managed to save her yet again, but this time she knew it wasn't just an accident, someone was trying to kill her.

17. The beach house was unusually quiet for a place hosting twelve people. She decided to check on the others but as soon as she got out of her room, she saw her husband mimicking for her to stay silent as he watched from the top of the stairs. One of the vacationers was lying in a pool of blood, and loud footsteps could be heard coming from the kitchen.

18. The floor creaked louder and louder as whoever was on the other side of the door approached her apartment. The first time after the break-in it was her boyfriend that gave her a scare, but this time he was with her and whoever was out there was definitely not a friendly face.

19. She must have been trapped in the cellar for days before the police found her. It was pure accident that she fell in love with the officer who saved her life back then, but now that she knew that the monster that kidnapped her was loose again, she wasn't sure if he was enough to protect her.

20. She had nowhere to run, but maybe that was a good thing. She was tired of running, and if she could just land one solid right hook in the murdering assholes face, maybe she could get an ambulance on time to save her boyfriend.

_____
_____
_____
_____
_____
_____
_____
_____
_____
_____
_____
_____
_____
_____
_____
_____
_____
_____

21. Falling for him was easy, it was keeping up with him that was hard. While she had her suspicions about his job being more than just a run of the mill bouncer, hired muscle wasn't what she had imagined. What's worse, the man he used to work for had it out for him now, and since they had gone public with their relationship last week, she had a target on her back too.

_____
_____
_____
_____
_____
_____
_____
_____
_____
_____
_____
_____
_____
_____
_____
_____
_____
_____

22. She ran across the road nearly getting hit by the sleek black car speeding down the road. A handsome man stepped out from the driver's seat, gave her his coat, and calmly walked her inside the car. It was the most kindness anyone had shown her in the last six months, but if he knew that a satanic cult was after her, he'd probably just leave her there without a second thought.

_____

_____

_____

_____

_____

_____

_____

_____

_____

_____

_____

_____

_____

_____

_____

_____

_____

_____

23. A bullet flew past her face as she ran across the parking lot. Of course, this would happen to her. She finally got a boyfriend, and it turns out he's a former hitman with more enemies than her socialite mother has fake friends.

_____

_____

_____

_____

_____

_____

_____

_____

_____

_____

_____

_____

_____

_____

_____

_____

_____

_____

24. Still grieving from her mother's recent passing, Maria decides a few days alone with her boyfriend in his family's remote cabin could do her some good. What she's not planning on is a serial killer stalking her there from the city, and with her boyfriend late to the party, can she survive long enough for him to get there?

25. The loud music and the hot guy she's dancing with are more than enough to take her mind off of her abusive ex, but when he goes off the rails and threatens to kill everyone in the building unless she shows her face, the handsome stranger might be her only hope of survival until the police arrive.

26. She didn't expect to be in a police chase with a random guy she met on a dating app tonight, but seeing as they were both at the wrong place at the wrong time, they'd have to clear their names together.

27. After the failed kidnapping attempt, Peggy and the best friend she's in love with try to find out who tried to take her and why. The only thing is, whoever it was, they haven't stopped trying since.

28. When Eli starts having suspicions that his frat is up to something more sinister than just hazing, he and his girlfriend attempt to connect their strange outings with the missing student reports on campus. Their investigation gets a bit more difficult when a man in a devil mask starts trying to put a wrench in their plans.

29. After Ava barely escapes an assault with her life, she and her boyfriend have to stay vigilant. There's a murderer in their quaint little college town, and if that's who attacked Ava, he'll come back to finish the job.

30. Time is ticking for Katherine. After waking up with an explosive device strapped to her waist, she has 48 hours to get rid of it. Going to the authorities will trigger it immediately, so instead, she goes to the only person she knows might be able to help - her hometown crush.

31. A hospital was the last place she wanted to be in, that's exactly where they'd look first. Still, if they didn't get her boyfriend's leg patched up, they'd never make it out of this mess alive. At least not both of them.

32. The bloody knife on the floor was a clear indication that he had found her. She just hoped the blood on the knife wasn't her husband's.

_____
_____
_____
_____
_____
_____
_____
_____
_____
_____
_____
_____
_____
_____
_____
_____
_____
_____
_____
_____
_____
_____
_____
_____
_____
_____
_____
_____
_____
_____
_____
_____
_____
_____
_____
_____
_____
_____
_____
_____

33. She could see her boyfriend trying to take the attacker down from the slightly ajar door. He managed to tackle him to the ground and follow suit, but with limited space in the hospital they were stuck in, they couldn't run for long.

34. She couldn't get too far with a broken leg, so hoping that a random stranger would stop and help her out was her only bet. By some miracle one did, and she was in shock both from how handsome he was and that she was finally safe. Of course, when a serial killer is after you, safe is a relative term.

35. With her throat damaged, he had to act as her mouthpiece. She prayed her boyfriend didn't mess up the speech because if he did, they'd have three different mob families gunning for their heads.

36. She felt strangely infatuated with the new guy at work, but she could also sense something off about him. Her curiosity got the best of her and she followed him home from work one day. Because of her one stupid mistake, they were now both stuck running from the organized crime ring he tried so hard to leave in his past.

_____

_____

_____

_____

_____

_____

_____

_____

_____

_____

_____

_____

_____

_____

_____

_____

_____

_____

_____

37. A fancy dinner date was one thing, but having the whole restaurant to themselves threw her for a loop. It all made sense when he told her what he did, and now she wished she had stayed away, knowing that his many enemies were hers as well.

_____

_____

_____

_____

_____

_____

_____

_____

_____

_____

_____

_____

_____

_____

_____

_____

38. She grew to be suspicious of knocks on her door after she survived being attacked by a serial killer. One look through the peephole and her worst nightmares materialized in front of her eyes. It was the same monster that had attacked her years ago, and next to her was the man she loved, the one who helped her get through it all.

39. She couldn't just have a romantic boombox moment like in the movies. No, her romantic moment had to come wrapped up in a murder mystery where she and her perfect guy were the main players.

40. Getting death threats by lunatics online was one big downside to being a professional gamer. A bigger one was when one of the same lunatics follows you and your boyfriend home for months in an attempt to deliver on them.

41. She feels the spiders crawl down her back, but her boyfriend is right there with his hand over her mouth to stifle her scream. If the invaders find out the house isn't empty, both of them are screwed.

42. There's something poetic about her and her husband being on the run from the police. They gave years of their lives in service, and now those they served with have turned on them because of dirty money.

---

43. Her claustrophobia had finally caught up with her at the worst moment. Here she was, stuck in a tiny elevator with a handsome man because of a break-in at the office, and all she could do was tremble.

---

44. In a moment of weakness, she goes back to him again. What she doesn't know is that he came went to something too, his old job as an enforcer for the mob, and now his old enemies were starting to catch up with him again.

_____

_____

_____

_____

_____

_____

_____

_____

_____

_____

_____

_____

_____

_____

_____

_____

_____

_____

45. The world around her was spinning. She could only hope now that her boyfriend would arrive at the bar in time for the first time in his life, or god knows what the monster that drugged her had planned.

_____

_____

_____

_____

_____

_____

_____

_____

_____

_____

_____

_____

_____

_____

_____

_____

_____

_____

_____

46. With no ride and no money, Kelly decides catching a ride back to New York with the cute hitchhiker she met isn't such a bad idea. They hit it off great, but the man who finally picks them up might not be as good of a person.

47. She can't remember the number of times she slipped and fell on the thick roots in the forest. These maniacs were hunting them for fun, and if she and the handsome man who found himself in the same predicament had a chance at making it out alive, they'd have to stick together.

48. She couldn't make out much in the dark, but she was sure that the killer had left the building by now. She knocked on her cute neighbour's door and got pulled in immediately with a hand stifling her grunts. "Shh. He's still out there."

49. The body in the lake was a gruesome sight, and they still had no idea who did it. She was sure it wasn't her boyfriend, they'd been together all night. That just left the twelve other people in a remote retreat in the middle of nowhere with a killer in their midst.

50. Her ex had left her with a broken heart and a ton of debt from his gambling addiction. Now, the assholes that fueled it have come to collect, and with no money, the only person she could call was the best friend she's been in love with her whole life.

---

50 Romantic Suspense Prompts

1.   Write about a girl who falls in love for the first time at summer camp. The problem is there's a killer on the loose, and it seems the one he's truly interested in is her crush.

_____

_____

_____

_____

_____

_____

_____

_____

_____

_____

_____

_____

_____

_____

_____

_____

2.   Write about a girl who falls for an ex-gambler. When his debts start catching up to him, they have to figure out a plan to pay them or end up at the bottom of the ocean.

_____

_____

_____

_____

_____

_____

_____

_____

_____

_____

_____

_____

_____

_____

_____

_____

3.   Write about a man who finds out his wife has a big secret. The family she's distanced herself from are founders of a suicide cult, and they've come to collect all former members for the final sacrifice.

4.   Write about a man who learns that the coworker he likes is a former adult movie star. He doesn't have a problem with it, but when their boss finds out, he goes into a maniacal rage and they're stuck in the crossfire.

5. Write about an exotic dancer who after years of not believing in love finds a boyfriend who treats her right. Things for them go well enough up until the point an obsessed former client of hers tries to tear them apart... literally.

6. Write about a market clerk and the cute customer she's flirting with. They start to hit it off when suddenly the store is invaded by robbers and they have to work together to find a way out.

7.   Write about the new girl in the friend group and the likable guy she falls for. Everything seems fine, but when their friends start mysteriously dying around them, they have to find out who's responsible before they get to them.

_____
_____
_____
_____
_____
_____
_____
_____
_____
_____
_____
_____
_____
_____
_____
_____
_____
_____
_____

8.   After a close call in a car accident, Riley develops a phobia of leaving the house. Write about the home invasion she lives through and the cute neighbour that helps her get the strength to escape.

_____
_____
_____
_____
_____
_____
_____
_____
_____
_____
_____
_____
_____
_____
_____
_____
_____

9.   Every day when the clock strikes midnight, one of their close friends ends up brutally murdered. Write about Dean and Jess, a couple who are tired of seeing their loved ones die, so they devise a plan to catch the murderer by becoming his next prime targets.

10. Someone is rummaging in the attic and Christie's home alone. Write about her journey of surviving a terrifying home invasion with just a baseball bat, her wits, and the constant support from her boyfriend on the phone.

_____
_____
_____
_____
_____
_____
_____
_____
_____
_____
_____
_____
_____
_____
_____
_____
_____
_____
_____
_____
_____
_____
_____
_____
_____
_____
_____
_____
_____
_____
_____
_____
_____
_____
_____
_____
_____
_____
_____
_____

11.   Write about a hostel where two strangers meet and have a whirlwind romance. In the middle of their newly established relationship, dead bodies start to pile up in the city they're visiting, and soon, they're faced with the man killing them himself.

_____

_____

_____

_____

_____

_____

_____

_____

_____

_____

_____

_____

_____

_____

_____

_____

_____

12.   The quaint town in rural Wisconsin gets a new sheriff. The Millers don't trust his friendly exterior, and once they start digging into his past, they realize the man's not the kind of hunter you usually see in these parts, but one that sees them as the best kind of prey.

_____

_____

_____

_____

_____

_____

_____

_____

_____

_____

_____

_____

_____

_____

_____

_____

_____

13. Through her teary eyes, Lena can see someone approaching the closet, but she's not sure if it's a friend or foe. Write about the worst night of her life and how her boyfriend attempts to save her from the stalker who's now broken into her home.

14. The parking lot is silent, but they know someone's moving around in the shadows. Write about how a young couple outsmarts a group of cultists that use young people as a sacrifice to the old gods.

15. There's no logical explanation behind Brian's reaction. By some intuition, he ducks his head and narrowly avoids the knife aimed at his head. Write about how he takes out a violent gang member that tries to kill him and continues to save his girlfriend from the former gang she was associated with back in her rebellious teenage years.

16. The mask he wears might look like a happy camper, but behind it is a cold-blooded killer. Write about the only couple that managed to survive the smiley-faced killer's massacre in the 1980s.

17. The knife flies right past her cheek and digs itself into the door. Surprisingly, she digs the knife out of the door and charges him ruthlessly. Write about the girl who managed to take down one of the most notorious serial killers in the world after almost murders her boyfriend in front of her.

18. Write about the lone survivor of an army mission in Afghanistan. His girlfriend helps him to try to move past what happened on the battlefield, but everything is not as it seems and an old friend now turned enemy is seemingly back from the dead to take away his happiness.

19. On a routine trip to work on the metro, couple Sienna and Lance end up trapped in a nightmare when the train stops and a group of terrorists walk in guns blazing. Write about their miraculous survival and their hand in helping stop the monsters before they were able to take even more innocent lives.

20. She's drowning again, but this time it's no accident. Write about the jealous best friend that has been plotting to kill Elena for years and the cautious boyfriend that somehow figures out what she's up to just in time.

21.   Their trip to the Caribbean shores turns deadly when a group of modern-day pirates tries to use them as drug mules back to the US. Write about two strangers that form a close bond in an impossible situation and manage to single-handedly bust out of a ship full of armed men and swim to safety.

_____
_____
_____
_____
_____
_____
_____
_____
_____
_____
_____
_____
_____
_____
_____
_____
_____
_____
_____

22.   After an unfortunate shipwreck, Theo and Lonnie end up stranded at sea on a small lifeboat. After days spent with only the two of them and the ocean, they start to develop feelings for each other, but they soon find out they're not the only hungry ones out there in the open water.

_____
_____
_____
_____
_____
_____
_____
_____
_____
_____
_____
_____
_____
_____
_____
_____
_____

23. With so much blood all over her, there was no way she wasn't going down for this murder. Write about a girl who finds herself in the wrong place at the wrong time, but thankfully, also finds the right kind of guy who could potentially get her out of this mess while simultaneously avoiding the police and keeping her sane.

24. Write about a girl that lives in a small town where nothing ever happens. She longs for adventure but gets more than she bargained for when she's thrown into a mass conspiracy that centres on the hot new guy who just moved to town.

25. Write about a singer who's secretly dating her high school sweetheart. When pictures of them kissing get leaked by the press, the couple finds out the hard way that some fans take celebrity obsession to a whole new deadly level.

26. Write about a couple that works as private investigators and the one case they could never solve coming back to haunt them.

27. Write about a high school student who goes to the town fair with her crush. They're stuck at the top of the Ferris wheel when all hell breaks loose below because of a terrorist attack.

28. Write about a girl who's being stalked by a crazy ex-boyfriend. When the restraining order doesn't work and he starts getting more aggressive, she decides to hire a bodyguard who she develops feelings for.

29.   There's a cannibal among them, and none of them have a clue who it could be. Write about Luna, a girl stuck in the aftermath of a wild party where a man was killed and eaten. She just hopes it wasn't the guy she hooked up with earlier.

30.   Write about a girl who's being stalked by a masked killer. The police think she's crazy, and so do her friends, but there's one person who believes her because he's also in the killer's crosshairs, the high school bully she secretly had a crush on.

31. Write about a luxury cruise ship that's taken over by a large group of gunmen. It just so happens that FBI agent Sarah is on that ship, and she has to work together with the handsome doctor she just met to turn the tide in their favour.

32. After Leona's article helps expose a crime ring, her life is in danger. Write about her journey to taking down their collaborators and the ditzy but adorable assistant that helps her do it.

33. Write about a group of tenants that band together to figure out the reason for the power outage in their building. When it turns out the source of the outage is more sinister than just faulty wiring, couple Diana and Ray need to keep a cool head and help everyone get through the night.

34. The world is in shambles as a deadly virus is quickly thinning down the population. Write about Gina, a scientist working on a cure with the lab assistant she's secretly in love with. They end up having a breakthrough, but the side effects might be even worse than the virus itself!

35. Write about Mary, a seemingly plain Jane that's unknowingly a sleeper agent. When one day she's awoken by a handsome man with a scar on his face, she knows her life is about to change forever.

---

36. After getting weird text messages for over a week, Lauren starts seeing a pattern. Write about her attempt at cracking the code and the hot hacker who helps her uncover the shocking secret behind what she's been receiving.

---

37. When Jared comes home from work, he sees his girlfriend broken down crying on the floor. Write about the reason behind her breakdown and the insane web of lies they have to weave to cover up the horrible mistake she made.

_____

_____

_____

_____

_____

_____

_____

_____

_____

_____

_____

_____

_____

_____

_____

_____

_____

_____

38. After a long dry spell, Tina is more than happy to listen to the hot random stranger that stops her on the street. Write about the concerning news he tells her and how both of them figure out their next steps together.

_____

_____

_____

_____

_____

_____

_____

_____

_____

_____

_____

_____

_____

_____

_____

_____

_____

39. All of her social media accounts were flooded by the threatening messages this anonymous monster was sending her, and then suddenly all of her personal info had been leaked out to the public. Write about Anna's journey to finding the hacker that's been ruining her life by getting the help of a gorgeous hacker of her own.

40. When she wakes up one day with her husband nowhere to be found, Veronica knows something's terribly wrong. Write about how she saves him from his obsessive family with dark secrets by pretending to be the perfect daughter-in-law.

41. Write about a woman whose husband mysteriously vanishes. It's not long before she finds him safe and sound with no recollection of what happened when he was missing, but the man that returned has a dark secret that soon rears its ugly head.

42. Write about a college student that's having an affair with her professor. They fall in love and he plans to leave his wife so they can be together, but when the wife sees them one day, she comes up with a meticulous plan for revenge.

43. Write about a college freshman that attends her first party. She hits it off with a guy who she likes a lot and sneaks off with him in private, but their little fling is cut short when they get blamed for the dead body in the pool.

44. Write about a woman trying to get over the death of her husband. After years she finally feels like she can move on with a great guy she meets, but their relationship is tested when a psychopath secretly starts putting reminders of her late husband everywhere around her.

45.   A beauty salon owner is put in an impossible situation. The mob wants to use her business as a front for a money-laundering scheme which is against everything she stands for, but if she doesn't agree, they'll make her life hell. Write about how she and her fireman boyfriend devise a plan to take them down with the help of their closest friends.

46.   Write about a killer who uses popular slasher movies as references to set up his murders. With Friday the 13th right around the corner, Nina and Cole find themselves face to face with someone in a hockey mask that seems very fond of axes.

47. Write about a couple that dresses up in grim reaper costumes for Halloween. They spot someone with the exact same mask as them at the massive rave they attend, but while they think it's a funny coincidence, their new acquaintance finds the issue deadly serious.

48. Write about a woman who finds out her husband is a foreign spy. He tells her he's left that life behind and what started out as a persona was now the only life he could imagine living because of her. As far as he knows, she's accepted his answer, but while she still loves him, she decides to do some digging herself.

49. Write about a couple that keeps hearing the same dripping noise every night they go to sleep in their newly bought home. After finally having enough, they go to the attic to check out what it is, but it seems it's not even close to the leaky pipe they had imagined.

50. It's a quiet night in the city up until people mysteriously start dropping like flies. Write about Erica and Manny, an unlikely duo that meets for the first time after witnessing the death of a mutual acquaintance. They work together to find out what's happening around them and start developing feelings for each other in the process.

CHAPTER SIX

100 HISTORICAL ROMANCE PROMPTS

In this section you will find four popular sub-sub-genres of Historical Romance writing prompts, including Ancient History Romance, Medieval Romance, Scottish/Highlander Romance, and Time Travel Romance (20th Century).

For each prompt, first think about:

Who is my character?
What is the setting?
What is the conflict?

25 Ancient Historical Romance Prompts

1. If she was being honest, the almighty Ra was kind of a dick. Luckily, he was easy on the eyes, and if there was ever a woman who could tame a god, it was her.

_____
_____
_____
_____
_____
_____
_____
_____
_____
_____
_____
_____
_____
_____
_____
_____
_____

2.   She saw him again when she went to leave offerings at Hera's Temple. She knew he wasn't fit to be her lover by everyone's standards, but she simply couldn't take her eyes off him.

_____

_____

_____

_____

_____

_____

_____

_____

_____

_____

_____

_____

_____

_____

_____

_____

3.   The chanting in the arena grew louder by the second. When she stepped out clad in armour fiercer than any man he had faced before, he thought he might spare her just to see what was hiding underneath it.

_____

_____

_____

_____

_____

_____

_____

_____

_____

_____

_____

_____

_____

_____

_____

_____

_____

_____

4.   Like all Gorgons before her, Medusa knew that no man would dare lay eyes on her again. That didn't stop her from dreaming. She followed her hero from a distance, hoping that one day by some miracle she would have the chance to be with him.

_____
_____
_____
_____
_____
_____
_____
_____
_____
_____
_____
_____
_____
_____
_____
_____
_____
_____

5.   The gods had blessed her with everything, beauty, intellect, and perseverance like no other woman before her. Every man she knew wanted to wed her, but the one she wanted had been sent to war years ago. She'd wait for him always, perseverance was her greatest blessings after all.

_____
_____
_____
_____
_____
_____
_____
_____
_____
_____
_____
_____
_____
_____
_____
_____
_____

6.   The Minotaur was running wild through the maze, trying to catch up to the deserter facing the punishment he deserved. She stepped in and gave him another chance, and by the gods, if there was one thing he knew was that he would never leave her side, no matter how bad things got.

_____

_____

_____

_____

_____

_____

_____

_____

_____

_____

_____

_____

_____

_____

_____

_____

7.   People always spoke of Egypt's unbearable heat, but they had no idea how cool the nights could get. Luckily, she had him by her side to keep her warm.

_____

_____

_____

_____

_____

_____

_____

_____

_____

_____

_____

_____

_____

_____

_____

_____

8. Her golden skin glistened beneath the moonlight as he ran his hand over her smooth back. The order of Anubis was right on their tail, but even if Anubis himself came to claim him, he'd never go without the woman he fell in love with.

_____

_____

_____

_____

_____

_____

_____

_____

_____

_____

_____

_____

_____

_____

_____

_____

_____

_____

_____

9. Her feet ached from the hot sands, but she had to accept that this was her life now. A slave only there to serve the next tyrant of a Pharaoh. She knew her strengths, and she knew she was beautiful, so if only she could get close to him, she might be the one to change everything once and for all.

_____

_____

_____

_____

_____

_____

_____

_____

_____

_____

_____

_____

_____

_____

_____

_____

10. When she was a girl, her mother would tell her stories of the dark prince Hades and his endless deceits. She had fallen for his charms anyway, and like the fool she was, she had given him her soul to use as a play toy.

---

11. Write about Pandora, who goes on a quest to put all the evils she released back into the box. She enlists the help of an arrogant hero, but the one who ends up helping, and the one ultimately falls for, is the hero's clumsy apprentice who after everything still holds onto hope.

---

12. Write about a gladiator who falls for the imperators soon to be wife. The two date in secret but when one of the other gladiators catches them in the act, they need to come up with a plan of escape immediately.

13. Write about an orphan girl who was raised by wolves in the Greek woods. The beautiful but savage young woman has lived most of her life in tune with the wild, but what happens when a philosopher stumbles onto her and tries to integrate her into society as his wife.

14. Write about a Roman archer who's never lost a fight in his life. During a battle with a tribe of new unexplored lands, he is bested by a fierce warrior. Humiliated, he makes it his mission to one day regain his dignity by defeating the beautiful woman who defeated him and making her his wife.

15. Write about a king's wife who'd do anything to give her husband a male heir. After many failures, she seeks help from Cercei, a powerful sorceress. Thinking her plan has worked the woman leaves happy, but instead of Cercei granting her the gift of a child, she casts a love spell on her that reveals the king isn't who she's supposed to be with, but a lowly infantry soldier instead.

16. Write about a cowardly man cursed by Zeus to wander the earth alone unless he makes the ultimate sacrifice for someone in need. His fear of almost everything makes him go on for years friendless and unloved, but when he sees a beautiful woman being attacked by some soldiers, he instinctively rushes in to help her, effectively changing his fate forever.

17. Write about a group of Spartan deserters that flee to the open sea and become pirates. Free from the strict regimen of his empire, their Captain Areus leads them to a new adventure, finding love along the way.

18. You've been accused of treason and you're on the run from the city's guards. Write about the thief that helps you escape the corrupt Roman Empire and the relationship that sparks between you while you try to clear your name.

19. Write about a philosopher who fiercely debates that morals should always be put above silly notions like love. He meets a free-spirited woman he can't help but be drawn to, and when he's put in an impossible place to decide between saving her life or the lives of endangered soldiers, he realizes he might have been wrong all along.

20. Write about an average man who seeks out help from the gods to save his dying wife. They tell him they'll grant him his wish only if he says the Hydra, but will he be able to do the impossible in the name of love?

_____

_____

_____

_____

_____

_____

_____

_____

_____

_____

_____

_____

_____

_____

_____

_____

_____

_____

_____

21. The flame in his eyes goes out, but she keeps on moving. It doesn't matter how many footmen the Pharaoh's armies kill, as long as they're not the man she loves, she'll keep on fighting.

_____

_____

_____

_____

_____

_____

_____

_____

_____

_____

_____

_____

_____

_____

_____

_____

_____

_____

22. Gold has never been enough to buy Sanura's affections, but when one day a handsome rogue shows up with a gorgeous ruby-encrusted scarab as an offering for her hand in marriage, she's not sure if she's more charmed by the token or the man offering it to her.

_____
_____
_____
_____
_____
_____
_____
_____
_____
_____
_____
_____
_____
_____
_____
_____
_____
_____
_____
_____

23. She dons her husband's armour and readies the sharpened sword. He might not be here with her to protect their home, but she'd rather die than let the men who nearly killed him invade the city she loves.

_____
_____
_____
_____
_____
_____
_____
_____
_____
_____
_____
_____
_____
_____
_____
_____
_____

24. Write about a newlywed Roman soldier who's sent off to war. He married his wife because of her family's status in the City, but when his fleet collides with a slave revolt, he can't help but betray her for the beautiful former slave that spares his life.

25. As per his usual routine, Zeus comes down to Earth to see how his loyal subjects are doing. Write about the beautiful woman he encounters in one of the poor villages and Zeus's approval of her selfless acts. Against all odds, he falls for her, but is it truly his place to stay on earth because of a silly crush?

25 Medieval Historical Romance Prompts

1.   The Queen had no qualms with working from the shadows, but if her husband thought he could limit her influence on the Kingdom she helped build, he had another thing coming.

_____
_____
_____
_____
_____
_____
_____
_____
_____
_____
_____
_____
_____
_____
_____
_____

2.   He was contempt with living out his days as a stable boy, but the runaway princess had other plans for him, ones that involved turning his back on the kingdom and never looking back.

_____
_____
_____
_____
_____
_____
_____
_____
_____
_____
_____
_____
_____
_____
_____
_____
_____

3.   Slaying a dragon was supposed to be his path to redemption. Still, no one told him that her human form would be that of the most beautiful woman he'd ever seen, so maybe being knighted again would have to wait.

_____

_____

_____

_____

_____

_____

_____

_____

_____

_____

_____

_____

_____

_____

_____

_____

_____

_____

_____

4.   The Arthurian legends failed to mention the spirit guiding Excalibur, nor did they mention how much the king longed to free her and make her his bride.

_____

_____

_____

_____

_____

_____

_____

_____

_____

_____

_____

_____

_____

_____

_____

_____

_____

_____

5.   She was engaged to marry a man she couldn't stand as to strengthen her Kingdom's alliances, but the man she truly loved had other plans, and her father had no idea of their planned escape.

_____
_____
_____
_____
_____
_____
_____
_____
_____
_____
_____
_____
_____
_____
_____
_____
_____
_____

6.   Magic was a rarity in England, but the ones that displayed signs of it were in for a bumpy ride. For Peggy, this made things even harder as her husband lead the order that was assigned to sniff sorcerers out.

_____
_____
_____
_____
_____
_____
_____
_____
_____
_____
_____
_____
_____
_____
_____
_____
_____
_____

7.   Enticed by his sweet words and rugged good looks, Princess Ella fell for a knight instead of a royal. Now both of them had a choice to make, stay together and get banished from their home, or stay apart and live out a life of eternal longing.

_____
_____
_____
_____
_____
_____
_____
_____
_____
_____
_____
_____
_____
_____
_____
_____
_____
_____
_____

8.   She clearly had the skills to take on an army by herself, but a female knight was simply unheard of. Despite it all, she decided to give it a try, and now all she had to do was impress the handsome but infamously stern general.

_____
_____
_____
_____
_____
_____
_____
_____
_____
_____
_____
_____
_____
_____
_____
_____
_____
_____
_____

9. A thief and a prince is a combo that generally doesn't work, but when Prince Aaron realizes the only way he can get his enchanted sword back is by working with England's most notorious thief, sparks fly between the unlikely duo.

10. As per usual, Emma's life was once again complicated by a handsome man. This time, it was her self-defence teacher, and unless she wanted to get in deep trouble with her father, the king, she'd have to keep up the poised princess act.

11.   The loud noises had spooked his horse, so now he was alone in the woods with nothing but his armour and sword. He would have thought that a weapon would keep the nymphs away, but it seems that one was so interested in him she was willing to risk it.

---

12.   As usual, they had arrived late at the castle. Her assigned date, the baron, was nowhere to be found, but maybe it was for the best as her favourite knight looked better than royalty tonight.

---

13. Her sword fell to the ground with a loud clank. In a last-ditch effort to protect herself from the enemy knight, she used her arms to cover her was, but a surprisingly gentle hand on her chin told her that maybe they weren't the monsters her King had made them out to be.

_____

_____

_____

_____

_____

_____

_____

_____

_____

_____

_____

_____

_____

_____

_____

_____

_____

_____

_____

14. Morgana was sick and tired of seeing her brother lead their Kingdom to its downfall, so she conjured the perfect killer to end Arthur once and for all. Unexpectedly, the killer wasn't as cold-blooded as the spell had intended, and once she fell in love with her creation, she decided she didn't give a damn about her Kingdom at all, she just cared for him.

_____

_____

_____

_____

_____

_____

_____

_____

_____

_____

_____

_____

_____

_____

_____

_____

_____

_____

15. In a desperate last effort to clear her name, Evelyn hires a young sorcerer to hex the crown into believing her when she says she's not a witch. The spell backfires, leaving both Evelyn and the sorcerer Wilmot on a wild run from the crown, where their feelings for each other get as tangled as the mess they've made.

16. Write about a knight who starts to display an affinity for magic. The problem is, he's a part of the anti-sorcery order in medieval England, and what's worse, he's having a secret affair with the magic hating Queen.

17. Write about a magic mirror that the king of England uses to spy on his enemies. It's helped him with dozens of battles, but when he lays eyes on the next enemy through it, he decided her country isn't the next conquest he's after.

_____

_____

_____

_____

_____

_____

_____

_____

_____

_____

_____

_____

_____

_____

_____

_____

_____

_____

18. Knighthood has been his dream since he was little, and when he gets in a tussle with a beautiful smuggler, he sees his chance for an easy way in. Write about his attempt to try to bring her in and the whirlwind romance that sparks between him, changing his life forever.

_____

_____

_____

_____

_____

_____

_____

_____

_____

_____

_____

_____

_____

_____

_____

_____

_____

_____

19. Write about the king's affair with a young peasant girl. She climbs through the social circles fast, and when she starts being a threat to exposing him, he needs to think of a way to get rid of her before the queen gets word of her.

20. Write about a wizard who advises the King on important matters. They grow close over the years but his infatuation with the king's daughter is threatening both his job and his comfortable life in the palace.

21. Write about a prince who wants anything but to ascend as the King of England. Looking for an adventure, he runs into a free-spirited knight who he decides to run away with.

22. On a hunting trip through the forest, the prince is attacked by a massive wild boar. Write about a poor but skilled archer who saves his life and their growing friendship that blossoms into much more.

23. Write about an evil witch that releases a plague upon England. In an attempt to thwart the curse, the king must work together with an old flame - the sorceresses Ellara.

24. Write about the classic tale of Excalibur, only this time Guinevere is the one who pulls the sword out of the rock, and both she and Arthur need to stop Morgan le Fay from leading the Kingdom into ruin.

25. Write about Merlin in his youth. The young wizard struggles with controlling his magic up until he meets Morgana, a troubled sorceress who he can't help but develop feelings for.

25 Time Travel (recent) Historical Romance Prompts

1.   Write about a man who accidentally time travels to a plantation a few years before the American Civil War. With the help of the resourceful young slave woman he falls for, they come up with an ingenious plan that's just risky enough to work.

_____

_____

_____

_____

_____

_____

_____

_____

_____

_____

_____

_____

_____

_____

_____

_____

_____

2.   Evan wasn't planning on ending up on the wrong side of the war when he traveled back in time. Still, using the knowledge he has of the future, he manipulates the Confederate leader Anna, a woman desperately in love with him, to turn the tide in the Union's favour.

_____

_____

_____

_____

_____

_____

_____

_____

_____

_____

_____

_____

_____

_____

_____

_____

3.   As a travelling circus performer you've seen the pain of being mistreated based on looks first-hand, so when by a turn of events you end up back in time to the Civil War, you decide to stand by the Union, the woman you unexpectedly fell in love with, and with doing what's right even if it kills you.

4.   With tensions only rising in the late 1800s in the USA, a young man decides to take to the seas and live out a life of solitude. That is until a strangely dressed, but albeit beautiful woman tells him he's the only man who can lead the country on the right path.

5.   The only way to get your family's secret recipe for the best burger in town now is to go back in time and learn it from the source itself - your great-great-grandfather. The problem is, once you get there the man refuses to give you a second glance, and what's worse, you seem to have developed feelings for a spunky journalist that thinks you're his next big story!

6.   You thought that flying a plane from the 1920s would be easy work when you traveled back in time to go for a joyride, but the outdated controls are a puzzle you simply can't solve. What's worse, the co-pilot you've been romancing for the last week seems to be an even worse pilot than you!

7.   Ally is sent back to the 1940s to research the first family that lived in the most haunted house in America. Things seem pretty normal at first, but when she starts getting intimate with the family's eldest son, he opens up to her about the voices he hears at night coming from the attic.

_____
_____
_____
_____
_____
_____
_____
_____
_____
_____
_____
_____
_____
_____
_____
_____
_____
_____

8.   You're sent back to 19th century California to dismantle an event with huge implications on current times. You land in the middle of a women's rights protest, and if that wasn't enough to get you to turn your back on the mission alone, the gorgeous speaker and her willingness to fight to drive the point home is.

_____
_____
_____
_____
_____
_____
_____
_____
_____
_____
_____
_____
_____
_____
_____
_____
_____

9.   Write about a man who's sent to prevent a mysterious murder in a fancy Manor in 19th century Boston. He gets side-tracked by the beautiful maid that he falls in love with, but what happens when he finds out she's the one who ultimately commits the deed?

_____

_____

_____

_____

_____

_____

_____

_____

_____

_____

_____

_____

_____

_____

_____

_____

_____

_____

10.   In an attempt to end a centuries-old feud between you and the family that lives on the farm next door, you travel back in time to where it all happened. Write about the scandalous secret you discover and the beautiful young woman who helps you unravel the web of mistrust between your two families.

_____

_____

_____

_____

_____

_____

_____

_____

_____

_____

_____

_____

_____

_____

_____

_____

_____

11. Write about a couple that rushes to get married before the husband is sent to fight in WW2. When he returns years later, he sees that his wife hasn't aged a day.

12. You travel back in time to Germany years before WW2 in hopes of stopping it from ever happening. Adjusting to the period is hard, but luckily, you've found an incredible girl who intends to help you with your mission.

13. Write about a man who loses an arm fighting in WW2. He struggles with coming to terms with his new normal, until the nurse tending to him shows him he's still good enough, especially for her.

14. You travel back in time to save your family line from the concentration camps. Write about the horrors you see while you're there and the beautiful girl who gives you hope for a better tomorrow.

15. Write about a scientist who travels back in time to research WW1 first-hand. He accidentally lands in the middle of the battlefield, but he's lucky enough to be saved by one of the few groups of brave women soldiers. His time travel gear damaged, he works with them closely to find a way back, but does he really want to after he falls for their fierce commander?

16. Write about a man who finds the horrific journey entries from a WW2 holocaust survivor. Through reading her story he falls in love with her, and armed with a time travel machine, he goes back in time to change things for the better.

17. Write about a woman who loses her husband in WW1 at the age of 22. She lives out the rest of her life miserable, but when on her 80th birthday she wakes up back in time to the day her husband left for the war, she does everything she can to keep him alive.

18. Anna doesn't want to follow Germany's inhumane new direction, but she has no choice but to stay silent. Of course, that is until a handsome man with strange clothing comes along and recruits her into his secret society against the Reich.

19. To save her great grandfather from his ill fate during WW2, Becca travels back in time. Write about her crazy journey and her even crazier love affair with her great grandfather's best friend.

_____
_____
_____
_____
_____
_____
_____
_____
_____
_____
_____
_____
_____
_____
_____
_____
_____
_____

20. Jane is sent back to WW2 to document the events first-hand. Write about her unfortunate landing into the opposition's hands, and her ultimate decision to stay in the past when she falls in love with the soldier who rescues her.

_____
_____
_____
_____
_____
_____
_____
_____
_____
_____
_____
_____
_____
_____
_____
_____
_____
_____

21. After finding her grandmother's love letters to a WW2 soldier she wasn't fated to end up with, Lola decides to travel back in time and relay the messages to him. The problem is, instead of giving him the letters, she falls for him as well!

22. When moving to her new apartment, Elsa discovers that the closet is a portal that leads to WW2 Paris. Seeking adventure, she dives right in, discovering love, adventure, and a new purpose in life - to better the future.

23.   Write about a woman who wakes up in Germany during WW2. She has no idea how she traveled back in time, but instead of looking for a way back, she joins the resistance where she meets the love of her life and uses her knowledge of the future to make sure the world has one.

_____
_____
_____
_____
_____
_____
_____
_____
_____
_____
_____
_____
_____
_____
_____
_____
_____
_____
_____
_____

24.   Write about an American housewife that sends her husband off to fight in WW2. Surprisingly, he returns only days later with a whole new wardrobe and years older, claiming he's been stuck in the future for 5 years!

_____
_____
_____
_____
_____
_____
_____
_____
_____
_____
_____
_____
_____
_____
_____
_____
_____
_____

25. Seeing his grandmother's pain over losing her husband back in WW2, Danny goes back in time to save him from the events that killed him, but when the time machine malfunctions, he gets sent into the fray of WW1 instead with only a gorgeous field medic as his guide.

25 Highlander Historical Romance Prompts

1.   With tensions between their two clans rising, Chief Neil knew what he had to do. The only problem was would his warrior of a daughter accept to be married to the enemy heir she's been fighting against her whole life?

_____
_____
_____
_____
_____
_____
_____
_____
_____
_____
_____
_____
_____
_____
_____
_____
_____
_____
_____
_____
_____
_____
_____
_____
_____
_____
_____
_____
_____
_____
_____
_____
_____
_____
_____
_____

2.   She might not have been a part of his clan, but every single touch of hers was worth losing everything over.

_____
_____
_____
_____
_____
_____
_____
_____
_____
_____
_____
_____
_____
_____
_____
_____
_____
_____
_____
_____

3.   The O'Donnell's had a choice to make, watch their clan fall apart at the seams, or accept the complete stranger their daughter brought into their folds and allow him to help.

_____
_____
_____
_____
_____
_____
_____
_____
_____
_____
_____
_____
_____
_____
_____
_____
_____
_____

4.   He ran into the forest after the girl. It was clear that she had trespassed into their territory, but he wasn't sure what he would do when he caught her. Someone that beautiful didn't deserve to face the Chief's wrath.

_____

_____

_____

_____

_____

_____

_____

_____

_____

_____

_____

_____

_____

_____

_____

_____

_____

_____

_____

5.   Mornings in the Scottish highlands were beautiful, but with how things were going this would be one of their last. If he wanted to give his wife everything she deserved, they'd have to go to war soon.

_____

_____

_____

_____

_____

_____

_____

_____

_____

_____

_____

_____

_____

_____

_____

_____

_____

6.   There's no place she'd rather be but home, yet with that manipulative monster as their chief, the burden of finding an appropriate replacement rests on her shoulders. Luckily, she knows the perfect man for the job - the man she loves.

_____

_____

_____

_____

_____

_____

_____

_____

_____

_____

_____

_____

_____

_____

_____

_____

_____

_____

7.   She can't make excuses anymore. She grabs her axe and dons her war paint. She'll do anything to get the love of her life back, even if it means taking on the entire McGregor clan by herself.

_____

_____

_____

_____

_____

_____

_____

_____

_____

_____

_____

_____

_____

_____

_____

_____

_____

_____

8. She rushed out onto the battlefield without absolutely no fear. Her husband was by her side, and when they were together, no clan stood a chance.

_____
_____
_____
_____
_____
_____
_____
_____
_____
_____
_____
_____
_____
_____
_____
_____
_____
_____
_____

9. With the English preparing to strike full force, their only chance was banding the clans together and working as a unit. This unfortunately meant being in close contact with his former flame now turned his biggest enemy - the Ewing Chief.

_____
_____
_____
_____
_____
_____
_____
_____
_____
_____
_____
_____
_____
_____
_____
_____
_____
_____

10. In her heart, she was a Conglinton, but that same heart was now telling her to follow a man from a clan that was once their biggest enemy.

11. Write about a girl who falls madly in love with a man she met in the forest. She finds he's a part of Clan Donald, the only problem, she's a member of clan Campbell - their biggest enemies.

12. Write about a girl who tries to dismantle the clan system and bring everyone together. She's met with resistance everywhere she turns, up until the chief of Clan MacKinnon falls in love with her.

13. Clan MacNeill has always been her family, but when she finds out her true origins come from clan Gregor, she vows to take revenge on the people who abandoned her. Write about her attempt at taking down a whole army and the handsome man who changes her opinion of the Gregor's.

14. In an attempt to seize the MacDonald's camp, she's outnumbered and captured by their men. Write about the traitor that releases her and her unexpected journey to save him from his clan.

15. The Maclean's always sought to take the most rewarding opportunities, no matter who they hurt in the process. Write about Harper, a man who teams up with an unlikely ally, his first flame, to take over the clan that's been led astray.

16. Write about a lowlands warrior who's banished into the highlands for refusing to kill an innocent British soldier. Instead of it being a punishment, he finds love with a girl who welcomes him into her clan.

17. Tensions inside the Gregor clan are rising over who should be the new Chief. Write about Shaw, a smart but physically weak man who, with the help of his lover, the Chief's daughter, tries to take over her father's seat.

18. While running from a massive wild boar, you trip and fall. Write about the handsome man that saves you and your promise to repay him by helping him fight off the lowlands clan that's after his family.

19. Write about Isla and Keith, a couple from two opposing clans that have been secretly seeing each other for months. Things don't seem so bad at first, but when word that Keith's father had killed Isla's brother reaches her, she has to decide whether she's fighting for love or revenge.

20. Write about Lachlan, a highlander whose only goal in life is to be the strongest warrior his clan has ever had. His aspirations start to pick up even more steam when he meets Skye, a beautiful warrior with similar goals.

21. Falling for an English soldier was the last thing she thought she'd do, but the reality of the situation was starting to set it. In her people's eyes, he was the enemy, but what was he in hers?

22. "I'm sorry..." she said with tears in her eyes as she drove her weapon into his side. "Don't worry, they'll never find out about us Blyth. I'll come back to you."

23. The lack of food was becoming more of an issue with each passing day for the Brodies. It was time to implement drastic measures to keep her clan afloat. It was time she married the wealthy man she could never love.

24. Write about the thinning members of Clan Durie. With nearly no resources left and their numbers dwindling, their leader Ailbert sets into the wild to ask for guidance from the gods but finds something better instead - a beautiful tree spirit that's willing to help.

25. Alec was never one for Clan politics, but when they decide to banish the girl he's been in love with since childhood for refusing to bear the Chief's children, he devises a plan to find her and bring down their straying brethren.

CHAPTER SEVEN

100 FANTASY ROMANCE PROMPTS

On the following pages are all sorts of Fantasy Romance story ideas and prompts. Here you'll find story ideas that include dragons, elves, more vampires, demons, and Angels.

For each prompt, first think about:

Who is my character?
What is the setting?
What is the conflict?

50 Fantasy Romance Story Starters

1.   Things were never supposed to last between them. A white Witch and a dark warlock getting together was unheard of, but if they could only stand up to their respective covens, then maybe there was a chance for them yet.

_____
_____
_____
_____
_____
_____
_____
_____
_____
_____
_____
_____
_____
_____
_____
_____

2.   The scarab lit up a bright green colour, revealing the not-so-mummified body in the tomb. Professor Anna Lynne wasn't sure what was more remarkable, the fact that she had brought a mummy back to life or that the mummy was the most beautiful man she had ever seen.

_____

3.   Walking into the vampire den was the easy part, her enchanted necklace provided more than enough protection against the bloodthirsty beings. Therein laid her conundrum. How was she supposed to get her captured vampire boyfriend out of there without the charm hurting him in particular?

_____

4.   She had her doubts about the new sorcerer in their school. Sure, all the other girls were going crazy over his looks, but she could see a darkness in his eyes and she knew she had to be the one to tame it.

_____

_____

_____

_____

_____

_____

_____

_____

_____

_____

_____

_____

_____

_____

_____

_____

_____

_____

_____

5.   "He's here, I can sense his magic." "Wait, what? How?" "We hooked up last week; don't make a whole thing out of it." "You slept with the werewolf we're hunting, what do you mean don't make a whole thing out of it!?"

_____

_____

_____

_____

_____

_____

_____

_____

_____

_____

_____

_____

_____

_____

_____

_____

_____

_____

6.   Lola's heart stopped when she saw the man she loves, the man she thought had just died falling over the cliff, rise up on a dragon's back and soar through the sky.

----

7.   It was silly of her to think that her grandmother would approve of her relationship with Ailon. He was just a commoner, and she was the next in line to ascend to the throne of the Elven Empire.

----

8.   She hated him with the same heat that she loved him. They'd come a long way since they were enemies, but even after their adventure on the Dragon Island a part of her still thought that he might just be using her.

9.   The greatest spell book was just within her reach. Money, power, eternal life... everything was right there, but she had a choice to make - save the man she loves, or get everything she's ever wanted.

10. For the first time in centuries, dragons filled the sky with their majestic dance. With her husband's hand in hers, they headed off into the new lands, knowing their purpose here was served.

11. She wrapped her hand around her engagement ring and smiled for the first time in years. When her fiancé went missing everyone was sure he had died, but now she knew he was out there, and her portal opening ring was going to lead her right to him.

12. Pyrokinesis was one of the strongest powers a person could wield, and her whole life everyone's only ever looked at her as a weapon. Then he came along and saw her for who she was. Now the fire inside of her burned bright enough to level a nation, and he didn't care about that part of her one bit.

_____
_____
_____
_____
_____
_____
_____
_____
_____
_____
_____
_____
_____
_____
_____
_____
_____
_____

13. The elf made a face of disgust as the humans passed by. He never reacted like that with her. She was the only human he could somewhat stand, and she was hopelessly in love with him.

_____
_____
_____
_____
_____
_____
_____
_____
_____
_____
_____
_____
_____
_____
_____
_____
_____
_____

14. The reasoning behind their plan was solid, but the one thing they didn't count on was how well their werewolf adversaries worked together. If they ever had a chance at beating them, they'd have to stop hiding their emotions and admit to each other that no matter how hard they tried not to, they had fallen in love.

_____

_____

_____

_____

_____

_____

_____

_____

_____

_____

_____

_____

_____

_____

_____

_____

_____

15. Her magical affinity was a birthright, but the immense power surge she got when he was near her was something else she couldn't put her finger on. If she was more of a believer in that sort of thing, she'd say it was their love that made her stronger.

_____

_____

_____

_____

_____

_____

_____

_____

_____

_____

_____

_____

_____

_____

_____

_____

_____

16. The more time she spent in the new world, the more the lines between her old life and new life blurred together. Suddenly, she wasn't sure of her relationship with Tom anymore, and her stunning warlock guide definitely wasn't making things any easier when it came to matters of the heart.

17. The ritual was supposed to be simple. They light a few candles, burn a flock of hair, say a silly chant, and everyone gets what they want. Seemingly, it worked too well. Her friends were living it up in Bali on their beds of money, while she was stuck with an insatiable incubus, the route to her deepest desires.

18. Leia met her guardian angel when she almost died in a car accident on her 18th birthday. The attraction between them was undeniable, but was their love worth the risk of breaking God's one rule for his messengers - never sleep with your ward?

19. Now that she was face to face with her greatest foe, Laura felt a different kind of tension between them than the one that stems from hatred. She was always one to go with what her instincts told her, and instead of putting a stake through the vampire's heart, she gave him a kiss that none of the trysts in his immortal life could ever compare to.

20. The well of souls in limbo seemed endless. She pushed through their screams to get to the one spirit she could never let go of - the man with whom she never got the chance to say "I do".

_____

_____

_____

_____

_____

_____

_____

_____

_____

_____

_____

_____

_____

_____

_____

_____

_____

_____

_____

_____

21. She was truly a vision in red, and the dim light of the nightclub didn't do her the justice she deserved. He gathered up the courage and pushed through the crowds to talk to her. Tonight, he'd go home with the Queen of the damned, and if she deemed him more worthy of being a snack than a date, then so be it.

_____

_____

_____

_____

_____

_____

_____

_____

_____

_____

_____

_____

_____

_____

_____

_____

_____

_____

22. "I mean it, Elliot! I'm not letting you go on that suicide mission alone!" "Why!? Why can't you just accept that this is how it was always going to end? I'm the only one who can stop the demon horde from taking over the city, even if it means sacrificing my life to do it." "Because I love you, you idiot! So we either go out together with a bang, or we hope that both of our powers combined are enough to let us fight another day."

_____

_____

_____

_____

_____

_____

_____

_____

_____

_____

_____

_____

_____

_____

_____

_____

_____

23. The moment she left the apartment, she knew she'd made a bad decision. Walking through the cursed city after midnight was always a bad decision, but lucky for her, she had a guardian angel looking after her - the night hunter who happened to be at the right place at the right time. The man she'd end up spending the rest of her life with.

_____

_____

_____

_____

_____

_____

_____

_____

_____

_____

_____

_____

_____

_____

_____

24. The trees whispered of the bad omens to come. She wasn't scared. In fact, she was thrilled about the impending doom coming to her doorstep. She had surpassed her demon-hunting boyfriend in nearly all regards in the last couple of years. With him and her new skill set at her side, kicking some demon ass was more than welcome.

25. No amount of training could have prepared him for this. The elves were supposed to be ruthless creatures who massacred everything in the way of their search for ancient magic. The beautiful Elven girl he'd met in his travels was neither ruthless nor obsessed with magic. She had the purest soul he'd ever seen, and he couldn't help but fall in love with her.

26. She wasn't expecting to fall in love with the man she couldn't stand just a few months ago, but then again, she also wasn't expecting him to save her life during a demon attack.

27. The orcs had been the fabled keepers of arcane magic through the centuries, and now the only magic left in their lands stemmed from a human girl who their chieftains' son was supposed to marry. It was a lot of pressure to put on the couple, but if things went well between them, the orcs might one day see wild magic everywhere as they had long ago.

28. "You're blocking my view!" "I'm blocking the fireball that's about to hit you in the face!" "Aww, thanks, babe." She leans in to give him a quick peck among the chaos. "Now get out-of-the-way, you're blocking my view."

29. She threw a snowball in his face and ran to hide behind a tree. It felt surreal to be here enjoying a peaceful winter morning with him after everything they'd been through, but even though she had lost a lot in the last battle against the invading undead, she was glad she gained a partner for life.

30. The snow giant tailing her was the least of her problems. If her boyfriend found out she had snuck out again to explore the forest outside of the castle, he'd break up with her for not inviting him to tag along.

31. Great, now she had a powerful Lich after her soul and her best friend, and secret crush for over five years was missing in action. She needed to set up a game plan. First, she scours the castle in hopes of finding Dan. Once she frees him from whatever's taken him hostage, they go after the Lich together, hoping that their joint power is good enough to take it down.

32. The troll made carefully practiced movements around her as if he was performing some sort of ritual. She wasn't the most well-versed in troll tradition, but if what she could remember was right, she was about to become the new blushing bride to the admittedly handsome troll she ran into in the forest.

33. He peeked inside the open portal, immersing himself in this new world full of magic. He was still hesitant to step inside, but that changed quickly when he saw the gorgeous elf sneaking behind the trees of the enchanted forest.

34. Dark clouds covered the sky as soon as the raven-haired man stepped onto the battlefield. She knew he was immensely powerful, and she knew that he was probably the only person who could pose a challenge to her in this war, but she couldn't help but get closer to him out of curiosity. Underneath that gloomy exterior, he was actually pretty handsome.

35. The name Darkhan was feared throughout all the lands and farther as far as she knew. She'd heard stories of him, of his cruel deeds and incredible dark power. That wasn't the man she saw standing in front of her now. She couldn't believe this pretty boy was the infamous Darkhan, and she couldn't help but let out a laugh when he offered her a bouquet of beautiful black roses.

36. A roll of thunder and a fierce lightning strike later, the God of thunder had landed on the open field where she had summoned him. She knew he was good-looking from what she'd seen in her books, but this was beyond anything she could have imagined.

_____

_____

_____

_____

_____

_____

_____

_____

_____

_____

_____

_____

_____

_____

_____

_____

_____

_____

_____

37. Iris rose up from her sarcophagus after thousands of years of being buried in the pyramid. She had made a deal with the gods that when the moon was just at the right angle, she'd walk among the world again under one condition - fair trade of a soul for a soul. The man in strange clothes that found her was seemingly the perfect sacrifice, but even with the ridiculous way he dressed and talked, she couldn't bring herself to end the life of someone she had developed feelings for.

_____

_____

_____

_____

_____

_____

_____

_____

_____

_____

_____

_____

_____

_____

_____

38. "There's nothing you can say that will stop me from going with him." "I love you, Luna". Luna was dumbstruck by the confession. What now? Should she go with the mysterious new vampire that turns everything into an adventure, or should she choose her best friend and stay in her comfort zone among the werewolves?

---

39. "That's the thing with you vamps, you always act like you're these untouchable beings with no emotions, but I can see through your façade." "Oh really, and what is it that I'm feeling exactly?" "Love." Betty mustered up the courage to get her lips as close to his as possible. The surprise on his face said it all.

---

40. Mimi couldn't get over the conflicting emotions in her heart now. The shapeshifter had killed her boyfriend and pretended to be him for over a year now and she hadn't noticed. Maybe it was because she wanted to believe that her boyfriend had truly changed his asshole ways, and real boyfriend or not, she couldn't deny that she had developed feelings for the being posing as him.

41. She knew dating a prince would be hard, but the constant intrigue that came with Elven society wasn't making things any easier. The newly arranged marriage between her boyfriend and the daughter of the army commander made her feel like the other woman, and she had no idea how to fix it.

42. She was always a "rules were meant to be broken" kind of girl, but this time she might have taken it too far by dating the voodoo queen's worst enemy - a common warlock.

43. She never stopped trying to see the good in everyone, which is why she gave the handsome warlock a chance when he asked for one. Now faced with a major demon with that same warlock, now her husband, at her side, she knew she had made the right decision by always following the light.

44. It took her months to decipher the alien language on the stone tablet they had uncovered on their last expedition. In a haze of sleeplessness and euphoria, she muttered the inscription out loud and was met with the only demon that'd ever spare her instead of killing her on the spot. He found her curiosity amusing, and she found his origins fascinating. It was a match made in hell.

45. The letters kept appearing in her locker every morning. She knew nothing about the sender, but the sender clearly knew too much about her. She'd have to nip this in the bud. If she wanted to protect herself from this anonymous and potentially telepathic threat, she needed to enlist the help of the one person she kept avoiding - her sorcerer ex-boyfriend.

46. She wasn't sure if she craved danger because of her harpy nature or because she had a lot of issues she needed to work through, but either way, it's what got her to date the Mafioso vampire she was doing a heist with. If her mother could see her now she'd have another heart attack.

47. The walls of the building kept disappearing, taking everyone in it with them. She wasn't sure what type of chaos magic was causing this, but she knew she needed to get to her boyfriend before their two completely opposite powers clashed and inadvertently started an apocalypse.

48. No one in the world had ever made her feel like that before. He made her feel safe and wanted, and if people couldn't accept the fact that he was half-demon, then she didn't need them anyway, she just needed him.

49. Thanks to a little sprinkle of fairy dust and a lock of werewolf hair, her love potion was complete. She released a few drops of the concoction into Dylan's drink, but it turned out it wasn't Dylan's drink at all! Now she was stuck with her childhood best friend making googly eyes at her all day, and surprisingly, she didn't mind it as much as she thought she would.

50. "You're the one they chose for the ceremony tonight." "But I don't even have the gift, why would they choose me?" "I heard the head sorcerer has a crush on you. Maybe that had something to do with it." "God, when will this nightmare end? I swear if I grow extra limbs I'm going to shove them up his..." "Ok, that's enough of that. Get ready, destiny awaits.

50 Fantasy Romance Prompts

1.   Write about a meek archeologist on an expedition in Egypt. She uncovers the hidden temple of the Sun God Ra and finds out he's not at all what she's read about in the myths. For one, he's much more attractive, and she can't help but be interested in him.

_____
_____
_____
_____
_____
_____
_____
_____
_____
_____
_____
_____
_____
_____
_____
_____
_____

2.   Write about a hidden lake that can make all of your dreams come true. A group of lost hikers accidentally stumble upon it, not knowing what it is, and they wake up the next day with true love knocking on their tents.

_____
_____
_____
_____
_____
_____
_____
_____
_____
_____
_____
_____
_____
_____
_____
_____

3.　Write about the young queen of a frozen wasteland. She must marry the king of a neighbouring tribe with more resources if she wants her people to survive, but he's not the man she's in love with, her army's commander is.

4.　Write about a girl who turns everything she touches to gold. One day she's kidnapped by a rogue set on using her gift for his own gain, but along the treacherous road to getting her back to his hometown, the two fall in love.

5.   Write about an angel that loses his wings after falling for a human. Now forced to live on earth, this former holy being has to adjust to modern-day life in NYC.

_____

_____

_____

_____

_____

_____

_____

_____

_____

_____

_____

_____

_____

_____

_____

_____

_____

_____

_____

_____

6.   Write about a sorceress whose spells always seem to have the opposite effect of what they were intended to do. She finds herself fighting a vampire, but instead of the curse she hexes him with killing him, it makes him fall in love with her.

_____

_____

_____

_____

_____

_____

_____

_____

_____

_____

_____

_____

_____

_____

_____

_____

_____

7. Write about a girl who sets out to find out the buried secrets in the tunnels under her city. She discovers that there's a whole other city down there where magical creatures roam freely, and she can't help but want to stay when she meets a charming werewolf.

8. New Orleans has been the nexus for magic on earth for centuries, but now the essence of magic is threatened by deranged Witch hunters who want to burn the whole city to the ground. Write about half-witch Leah and her human husband who are the last hope of stopping that from happening.

9.   Write about Kelsey, a half-demon who has to choose between her life on earth with the love of her life, or the throne of hell where she would reign supreme over the underworld.

_____

_____

_____

_____

_____

_____

_____

_____

_____

_____

_____

_____

_____

_____

_____

_____

_____

_____

_____

_____

_____

10.   Magic is out of sorts, and no one knows why. Write about Mona, a witch who suspects her crush might be the one sabotaging magic after she sees him making a deal with the Prince of Hell.

_____

_____

_____

_____

_____

_____

_____

_____

_____

_____

_____

_____

_____

_____

_____

_____

_____

_____

_____

11. On their sixteenth birthday, all mermaids are granted legs for a week so they can experience life on land and choose between it and the sea. Write about Eva, a mermaid who in seven short days finds a boy who might be worth giving up her tail for.

_____
_____
_____
_____
_____
_____
_____
_____
_____
_____
_____
_____
_____
_____
_____
_____

12. It's the first blood moon in nearly a decade, and as a witch, Layla's powers are amplified greatly. Write about her finally having the power to cast the spell that will find the man she's in love with, the man who saved her from a werewolf attack seven years ago.

_____
_____
_____
_____
_____
_____
_____
_____
_____
_____
_____
_____
_____
_____
_____
_____

13. Diana never felt like she belonged, and realized why when she stumbled upon a vampire massacre on her way home from work one night. She wanted to be scared, but the leader of the vampire gang looked great in a leather jacket, and all she could think about was him sinking his teeth into her.

14. Write about a man who uses the fountain of youth to bring his wife back from the dead. Against all odds, it works but is the woman who came back truly his wife or an imposter he can't help but have feelings for.

15. On Halloween, all the ancient deities visit earth for a day to mingle with the humans. Write about The God of Forests Oren, who's thrilled about the festivities, but gets more than he bargained for when a beautiful human girl dressed as a nymph tries to assassinate him.

16. Write about a girl with the power to clone herself. She uses her powers to never fall behind on anything, but when two handsome boys show up at her door claiming they've been dating her for months, she realizes that some of her clones might have a mind of their own.

17. Write about an elven prince whose sole focus in life has been looking after his Kingdom, and the free-spirited nymph who teaches him there's more to life than strategy meeting and diplomatic talks.

18. Write about a demon hunter who falls for the devil's daughter. She's not like any demon he's ever met before, but should he trust his rational mind and run in the opposite direction or take her hand and see where things take them?

19. Write about Niri, a warrior that keeps her boyfriend's soul shard in the hilt of her blade, and her peril wrought journey to freeing it so they can be reunited again.

20. The clock strikes midnight and Lonnie's powers are finally freed. Write about this witch's road to revenge on the men that bound her powers, and the only person in the world who has a chance of stopping her before she crosses a line she can't come back from - the ex-boyfriend she's still in love with.

21. Write about a King whose land is threatened by an enemy state. In order to protect his people, he has to make a sacrifice he'd been hoping to avoid - marry the neighbouring orc chieftain's daughter.

22. Write about a girl who can see ghosts. She's helped them cross over to the other side her whole life, but when she meets Ryan, the spirit of a soldier who died serving in South Korea, she tries to do everything to keep the ghost she's fallen in love with from crossing over.

23. Write about a human servant who's secretly in love with the Elven princess he works for. He doesn't think he stands a chance with her, but the subtle hints she's been dropping lately say otherwise.

24. Write about Elise, a warden in the highest security prison in the world. She's been tasked with watching over one of the most powerful dark sorcerers to ever walk this realm, but over the time she had gotten to know him, she'd fallen in love with him. Now she's faced with a decision, step off her duties and move on, or help him escape and hope for the best.

25. Write about a powerful sorceress who trades her magic for something much more important - her husband's life. Now a mere human, she and her husband have to find a way to destroy the demons that took him and her extremely dangerous powers.

_____
_____
_____
_____
_____
_____
_____
_____
_____
_____
_____
_____
_____
_____
_____
_____
_____

26. Write about a fox spirit that uses magic to transform into a beautiful woman. She wanders the outskirts of the city observing the humans but never approaches them. Until one day, she sees a handsome merchant, that is.

_____
_____
_____
_____
_____
_____
_____
_____
_____
_____
_____
_____
_____
_____
_____
_____
_____
_____

27. Write about a girl who discovers that the best friend she's secretly in love with is a werewolf. She's shocked at first, but decides she wants him to turn her so she can be with him.

28. Write about a wizard who manipulates a powerful witch into giving him his powers. Now armed with three demon brothers, one of which she's dating, she's on the warpath to take back what's rightfully hers.

29. Write about a girl whose nightmares keep coming to life for short periods. After a string of horrifying events that she barely makes it out of, she dreams of the perfect man. She's shocked to find him in her bedroom the next morning, but how long before this dream fades away too?

30. Write about a giant who's in love with a human girl. Their love can never be, but when he seeks out an old hag that claims she can turn him human for a price, he takes the chance in a heartbeat.

31. Write about a young shaman in training who's asked to help heal a wounded enemy soldier for questioning. He manages to successfully heal the soldier, but while waiting for the army to pick her up, he sees things from her point of view and decides to free her and run off together instead.

32. Write about a girl with the power to transform into a cougar. She's never met anyone like her before, but one night while giving in to her primal side and hunting in the forest, she meets another shifter that she can't help but feel drawn to.

33. Write about Ari, a seamstress who's unaware that her dresses make anyone that wears them irresistible to the opposite sex. She's never felt comfortable wearing her own designs, but when one day in a hurry for a job interview she throws on the first dress she finds in her closet, she gets the job of her dreams, and the handsome boss as a bonus.

_____

_____

_____

_____

_____

_____

_____

_____

_____

_____

_____

_____

_____

_____

_____

_____

_____

34. At midnight on Halloween, the veil between the world of the living and the dead is lifted, causing chaos to erupt all over the globe. Write about Max and Tara, a newlywed couple dressed as zombies who manage to survive the night of the living dead thanks to their ridiculous costumes.

_____

_____

_____

_____

_____

_____

_____

_____

_____

_____

_____

_____

_____

_____

_____

_____

35. The guy you've dated for three months now has just revealed he's a vampire. Write about your journey to accepting what he is and the wild introduction to a darker side of the world most people didn't know existed.

36. Write about Sam, a shapeshifter who uses her powers to appear beautiful so she can always get her way. That all changes when she meets a sorcerer who can see right through her glamour but chooses to pursue her, anyway.

37. Write about an organization that wipes the minds of their powered agents after every mission and brainwash them to keep them complacent. Red is sent to assassinate a woman she's been told is an organized crime lord, but when a good-looking mystery man foils her attempt and takes her for a stroll through town, she starts remembering some of the dark pieces of her life that were erased.

38. Write about a sorcerer whose wife leaves him out of the blue. He's angry and confused at first, but when he finds that she has a massive bounty on her because of her past, he realizes she was only trying to protect him. Now, it was his turn to protect her.

39. Write about a private investigator hired to find a missing person. His search for the beautiful college student leads him to the discovery of New York's supernatural underbelly, where he falls for his case in the process of trying to save her from a vampire cult.

40. Bonnie has the power to stop time. One day while trying to cheat on a math test, she notices that the cute new guy at school isn't affected by her powers. Write about why that is.

41. Write about the warring Elven tribes of Elk. They've been at throngs with each other for centuries, but could the unforeseen love between two soldiers from opposite sides of the war be the catalysts for change?

42. Write about a night hunter that gets an assignment to kill a Witch. In the three months he's been tracking the elusive Witch, he fails to finish the task, so he decides to try a different way to get to her - seduction.

43. Write about Alune, an Angel who in the middle of a heated battle between angels and demons falls from grace down to Earth. He lands directly into the dorm room of a shy and quiet college student. While he helps her break out of her shell and she helps him get adjusted to living among humans, the two fall in love.

44. Write about a world where the roles of monsters and humans are reversed. One night during Dracula's deep slumber, his sleep is disturbed by a human visiting his castle. He freaks out at first, but after spending some time with her, he realizes humans might not be so bad after all, especially the ones that look that good.

45. Write about a man who was cursed by a witch to never find true love. He spends his days isolated from others, only going to work at his cushy office job. One day a beautiful temp joins the firm and brings back the joy in his life, but what does it all mean if the curse is still active?

_____
_____
_____
_____
_____
_____
_____
_____
_____
_____
_____
_____
_____
_____
_____
_____
_____
_____
_____
_____

46. Write about a spoiled prince who's been exiled from his kingdom. He travels the lands trying to find himself, barely scraping by in the harsh condition of the real-world he was sheltered from. At the moment he thinks it's time to give up he meets Kat, a scrappy rogue who might be exactly the thing he's been looking for.

_____
_____
_____
_____
_____
_____
_____
_____
_____
_____
_____
_____
_____
_____
_____
_____
_____
_____
_____

47. Write about a girl who conjures up a ghost by accident. He's annoying, rude, and a shameless flirt, but when she hires a witch to do a banishing ritual, instead of getting him to move on she gives him a corporeal form.

_____

_____

_____

_____

_____

_____

_____

_____

_____

_____

_____

_____

_____

_____

_____

_____

_____

_____

48. Write about a rare virus that gives people special abilities. Drew and Angela were both infected, gaining the powers of super strength and flight. It all seems great at first, but when a government organization intent on capturing them for their research starts relentlessly hunting them; they only have each other to rely on.

_____

_____

_____

_____

_____

_____

_____

_____

_____

_____

_____

_____

_____

_____

_____

49.   You have three months to find the love of your life or the demon of lust Inaccus will drag you down to hell with him. Write about your frantic search for the man of your dreams and the many failed attempts along the way.

---

50.   Your sorcerer boyfriend's been possessed by an evil spirit. Write about your attempt to stop him from causing chaos and your search for one of the rarest old world spells in existence - an exorcism.

CHAPTER EIGHT

SUMMARY

I hope you enjoyed these romance writing prompts. Don't forget, just use what you want, and you never have to use the whole prompt. Even blend the prompts if you like.

If you'd like more prompts, check out thebusywritersnotebook.com, where I have new writing prompts each month.

Sign up for my mailing list to be notified when new prompts are posted, and when I have a new writing prompt book out. Sign up at https://bit.ly/2JbLa6o, and you'll receive a bonus 30 Epic Fantasy Prompts!

If you enjoyed this book, I'd really appreciate it if you could leave me a short review on your favourite platform. I'd love to hear your thoughts and feedback.

Happy Writing!

Erica

ABOUT THE AUTHOR

Erica Blumenthal is a long-time lover of science fiction, fantasy, old school dystopian fiction and apocalyptic fiction, and more recently urban fantasy. Erica writes under the pen name Candence Stone, and is currently working on her first YA Fantasy series.

She blogs about writing, writing resources, and writing prompts at thebusywritersnotebook.com.

She has a Masters of Science in Geology, and currently lives in the South West of WA in Australia with her daughter and partner.

Made in the USA
Las Vegas, NV
29 April 2023

71306451R00171